Dr George Sik is a psychologist and w[illegible] the study and assessment of personality, both at work and in sport. As well as giving frequent talks and lectures, he contributes regularly to newspapers and magazines, including *FourFourTwo*, *The Pyschologist* and *90 Minutes*, and has made numerous television and radio appearances.

A keen football fan, he follows Newcastle United but says he will happily go and watch anyone play (with the obvious exception of Arsenal).

In 1987, he achieved minor notoriety by becoming the first psychologist ever to appear on 'Blind Date'.

I Think I'll Manage

Football Managers Reveal the Tricks of Their Trade

George Sik

HEADLINE

For my friends

First published in 1997
by HEADLINE BOOK PUBLISHING

First published in paperback in 1996
by HEADLINE BOOK PUBLISHING

10 9 8 7 6 5 4 3 2 1

ISBN 0 7472 5294 7

Typeset by
Letterpart Limited, Reigate, Surrey

Printed and bound in Great Britain by
Cox & Wyman Ltd, Reading, Berks

HEADLINE BOOK PUBLISHING
A division of Hodder Headline PLC
338 Euston Road
London NW1 3BH

Contents

Acknowledgements

I'd like to thank everyone who made this book possible. In particular, I'd like to record my appreciation for the ideas and energy provided by my friend and colleague Stevie Smith (Celtic) with whom I followed Scotland in the 1992 European Championship in Sweden, and will be doing so again in 1996, my agent, Jonathan Harris (QPR), Ian Marshall at Headline (Manchester United, alas) and Martin Fiddaman (Spurs), without whose thirtieth birthday party Jonathan and I might never have renewed our acquaintance.

My gratitude also goes to my family (Sparta and Slavia Praha), who have always encouraged me in what I do and have given me invaluable support. Thanks, Mum, Dad and Joan!

Among other psychologists, an interest in football can lead to sneering condescension, but some of the biggest names in the field have given me their support and their advice over the years, particularly Prof. Peter Saville and Dr John Nicholson (both QPR) as well as Prof. John Morton (Burnley).

I'd also like to thank my friends for those drunken Saturday-night-after-the-match post-mortems that have done so much to focus my ideas, secure in the knowledge that the more of them I mention, the more people are likely to buy this book. Martin

Shillingford, Dave Bere and Steve Reddaway will probably never forgive me for turning my back on Spurs when I acquired an allergy to Sugar. John Kirkpatrick, Paul Rodwell and Alex St Julien showed me the light (Toon Toon!) thanks to an elaborate ceremony featuring bottles of Newcastle Brown and a photograph of Andy Cole (now persona non grata). Many other friends have joined me at matches or given me other help, who simply have the misfortune to follow the wrong team: Alex Pearce (Liverpool); Neil Cowieson (Liverpool); John Leah (Manchester City); Paul West (Exeter); Paul Earland (Portsmouth); Jason Hopperton (Nottingham Forest); Craig Gibson (Rangers); Billy Brewster (West Ham); Martin Lloyd-Elliott (Chelsea); Tony Borkowski (Fulham); Simon Halls (Brighton); Stuart Clement (Celtic); Jim Donaldson (Rangers); Lee Campbell (Manchester City); Rab MacIver (Rangers); Steve Gibson (Manchester United *and* Rangers – talk about obvious!); Patrick Gibbons (never one to go all nationalistic on you, but the Republic of Ireland); Anne Pelan (Distillery – this is only a guess, but it seems the most appropriate Northern Irish team) and Phill Bamford (Urgh! Arsenal! And he even *looks* like Nick Hornby). Matt Goff (Brentford) and Stuart Copus (Southend) have not only been hugely supportive, but continue to work at the cutting edge of psychological research in football – keep it up, lads!

The managers interviewed here gave up their time and opened up their hearts, and I'd like to thank them all. Indeed, they more or less wrote the book for me! Thank you to: Mark McGhee (Wolverhampton Wanderers); Tommy Burns (Celtic); Walter Smith (Rangers); Dave 'Harry' Bassett (Crystal Palace); Alan Smith (Wycombe Wanderers); Joe Kinnear (Wimbledon); Jim Smith (Derby County); Frank Murphy, Johnny Johnson and the footballing Chippendales of Dulwich Hamlet, where Russell Edwards is, I'm sure, set to be a manager of the future; and, of course, Terry Venables and indeed everyone at Scribes, where I've spent many a happy Saturday night.

Additional thanks to Judie Welsted (West Ham) for taking calls when I was away, Lesley Randall for running my highly exclusive fan club (she is currently the only member since the annual subscription went up to 20p) and Elizabeth Beresford, whose kind words encouraged me to persevere with writing (as the creator of *The Wombles*, she'll be delighted to learn that this book has not one but *two* Wimbledon managers in it!).

Last but certainly not least, I'd like to thank Chris Clement (Rangers), my minder in the dangerous, cutthroat world of professional psychology, a worthy Terry McCann to my Arthur Daley, for reminding me, when this book threatened to become too much of an obsession, that there is more to life than football. There is also boxing.

Preface

'If Kenny Dalglish has resigned because of the pressures of the job, the rest of us have no chance.'

Howard Wilkinson, 1991

The cult show *Fantasy Football League* used to begin with its presenters, Frank Skinner and David Baddiel, sitting in front of the telly watching another dismal England performance creak to its inevitable conclusion. The national side had flopped again and the commentator's words reflected the gloom and despondency of the occasion: 'Who'd be a football manager?'

At this, a flicker passed across both presenters' expressions as they contemplated the idea of being football managers and, just as in the adverts for Hamlet cigars, broad grins spread slowly across both their faces as they punched the air, simultaneously mouthing 'YES!'

It was a splendid opening, echoing the feelings of most of those who love football about managing their own team. It's every fan's dream . . . every fan's *fantasy*. Fantasy football spread like wild-fire, thanks largely to leagues run in *90 Minutes* magazine and the *Daily Telegraph*, with practically all the other papers in hot pursuit, cashing in on this latest craze. The idea was simple: you 'buy' a bunch of players, and you get points depending on the real performance of those players week in, week out in the Premiership. If 'your' player scores or assists, you get rewarded; if 'your' defender or keeper concedes goals, you get penalised. The idea was beautiful in its simplicity. Up until then, such fantasy leagues had been the hobby of 'football anoraks', portrayed so vividly in the television programme by cult hero Statto (in reality, a Eurosport commentator). Suddenly, the whole country was at it – over three hundred thousand people took part in the *Daily Telegraph* league alone! It seemed everyone wanted to be a football manager.

Ah, but did they?

In this age of leisure, the entertainment industries work overnight to satisfy our wildest fantasies. Video games enable us to do anything from piloting an aircraft to playing pinball with a live hedgehog (presumably for those who haven't tried either of these things for real). We can go on Murder Mystery Weekends, or, if we are particularly sad, indulge in Dungeons and Dragons games of sword and sorcery. But these are *fantasies*. Taking part in fantasy football is all very well for David Baddiel, Nick Hornby and others who have got what it takes, but picking a 'squad' of individuals who we think are about to have a good season has little to do with the experience of managing a *real* football team. No one wins a game of Monopoly and walks away thinking that they would be a good property speculator as a result. No one joins the police on the strength of being a Cluedo champion. If you walked into your local Army recruitment office and told them that you're a general in the making because you've always been good at Risk or Campaign, they'd laugh in your face (they'd sign you up anyway, of course – they're desperate these days). In the same way, there's inevitably going to be more to being a football manager than selecting a bunch of players who you think are on a roll.

One of the most disturbing things I have seen in a televised match was the expression on Jock Stein's face immediately prior to his fatal heart attack during the game against Wales which led to Scotland's qualification for the final stages of the 1986 World Cup. Stein lived for the game and is rightly acknowledged as one of the finest managers of all time. He was desperate that Scotland should qualify and his final wish was granted – but at what price to him? Did the stress of the job contribute to that coronary? There's a lot of discussion in the media about stress levels in various professions. Psychologists once identified the most stressful occupation as that of a racing driver, but a football manager can't be far behind: all that adrenaline, the heart pumping away, the palms sweating . . . And what can you do about it? Can you run around a little to calm yourself down? No, you have to sit quietly on the sidelines – and if your stoicism slips, you face a touchline ban! We hear all the time of managers having heart murmurs or triple-bypass surgery, ulcers, angina, unusually high blood pressure: all the psychosomatic symptoms of a high-stress job. When Kenny Dalglish resigned as manager of Liverpool, it was the stress of the job that caused him to make his decision. Many managers empathised.

Who *would* be a football manager?

Well, some people evidently would. This book is a tribute to them.

Dr George Sik, July 1995

Introduction

'It's not like the brochures.'

Kevin Keegan at the start of his management career, 1992

I'm sure it's not. But what *is* it like to be a football manager? This is a record of my one-season mission to find out what I could.

I decided to follow a season through the eyes of a group of football managers, finding out how they saw issues affecting their own clubs and others, through good times and bad. It could have been any season. All that really differs as you drift through time is the music and the hairstyles. The more people say football has changed, the more I think that the people at the heart of the game haven't altered that much. They still get excited about the same things, still feel the passion associated with the nation's – and most of the world's – favourite game. They still feel the bitterness of defeat and the glory of victory. With so much money now floating about in the game, creating additional pressures, they probably feel it more.

For my managers, I chose to approach a select few, ones I tended to admire myself for one reason or another (as distinct from the feelings towards particular teams which being a supporter can inflame). I asked to speak to them early on in the season and then have the chance to phone up occasionally as the season progressed, should incidents occur which needed comments. I was very pleased with the response. Those who either declined to be interviewed or didn't reply at all could be counted on the fingers of one hand. I had been able to attract what I feel makes a very realistic cross-section of what's out there.

Terry Venables is, for my money, one of the best – if not *the* best. The papers always had a habit of going on at great length about who he should or should not be selecting, as flavours of the month (Andy Cole, Matt Le Tissier) came and went, but few could recommend a man better suited for the top job, that of Chief Coach of the England squad. It was an open secret that he did not enjoy managing the national team as much as he enjoyed club management, and could have done with more support from sections of the Football Association, but was nevertheless determined to give it his best shot. With all its stresses and strains, was the job of England manager really impossible, as Channel 4's documentary about Terry's predecessor claimed? Or would he end up surprising his doubters in '96?

Dave Bassett took Wimbledon from nothing to the top flight, assembling a side that later went on to beat Liverpool in the 1988 FA Cup Final. Wimbledon, while obviously a technically inferior side, had shown everyone what effective management and a strong team spirit can achieve. He is something of a maverick and one of the most outspoken figures in the game.

Current manager Joe Kinnear keeps that team spirit going, to the point where far richer clubs often ask Wimbledon, 'What's your secret?' He is the embodiment of the club's 'Crazy Gang' spirit and, as the season started, was widely tipped as a possible manager of the Irish national side on Jack Charlton's retirement.

The Old Firm of Rangers and Celtic Football Clubs makes Glasgow probably the most vibrant football city in Britain. In the late sixties and early seventies, Celtic always won everything. Now the boot is on the other foot and Rangers always win everything. Their boss, Walter Smith, took over from the charismatic but hugely controversial Graeme Souness. Under Smith, Rangers have dominated Scottish football, but struggled in European matches. Would this year prove the exception?

Across Glasgow to the East, Tommy Burns presides over Celtic. There is no doubt that he bleeds green and white. Even when he was cutting his managerial teeth at Kilmarnock, everyone knew that Lou Macari was just keeping the seat warm for him. Burns' return to Celtic, where he was one of the club's most popular players, spelled a new optimism among fans of a club torn apart by boardroom unrest.

Mark McGhee, another former Celtic favourite as a player, is still relatively new to management but, at the beginning of the season, had already enjoyed great success at Reading. One of the fresh breed of successful young gaffers who made the move into management straight from playing, without the traditional intermediate steps of coaching, he began the season at Leicester City, a club with a good chance of promotion into the Premiership. In the club shop they sold T-shirts depicting a picture of him as Highlander, brandishing a claymore high above his head. 'There can only be one!' they proclaimed.

Jim Smith had just taken over at Derby County. His appointment did not cause dancing in the streets, but he brought with him a wealth of experience gained at other clubs including Portsmouth, Newcastle and QPR. His nickname 'The Bald Eagle' may be a reflection on a career where relationships with chairmen have not always been smooth, and where tearing your own hair out may be all too natural a reaction.

Alan Smith was one of Crystal Palace's most popular managers and had just taken over the reins at Wycombe Wanderers. The acrimonious relationship between Palace's manager and the club chairman, Ron Noades, has been documented extensively in the papers, but Smith is remembered with great affection by many of the players who started out at the club. Relatively unusually by football standards, he has been a successful businessman quite apart from his managerial career.

Frank Murphy is the player-manager at non-league Dulwich Hamlet, one of the most exciting sides of the ICIS Premier League (formerly the Isthmian League, or the Diadora League, as they were known last season), whose champions, in theory at least, can get promoted into the Vauxhall Conference. Murphy acknowledges that his is a club fuelled by team spirit and modestly gives most of the credit to his players. At thirty-six, he tends to manage more than play these days, and smiles more often than certain better-known Scottish managers one could mention.

I didn't want to include some of the ultra-successful club managers of the modern game, the Dalglishes and the Fergusons, in this book, mainly because so much has been written about them already. They have whole books to themselves, allowing us to find out a great deal about their styles. I was aiming for a group of managers who represented football at every level, ones with perhaps a bit of a reputation for speaking their minds or with stories to tell, and, as it turned out, that's exactly what I ended up with. Some of those I approached have actually changed clubs since agreeing to take part.

I tried to ask questions which might have been asked many times before in different ways, and maybe throw in a few that the managers had rarely, if ever, been asked. Though a psychologist by profession, I didn't want those managers taking part to feel they were 'on the couch' or being asked to reveal deep, dark secrets against their will. What I was after was an honest, upbeat (difficult at certain points in the season!) and enlightening chat, of the sort that any fan might have if he had a couple of hours to talk to a football manager over a pint.

Occasionally, I'd ask a manager whether he wanted anything taken 'off the record' – you can get carried away if you've been talking a long time. They never did. The nearest any of them came to a request for censorship was when one asked me to 'leave some of the "fucks" out, if you could'. Not being Jackie Collins, I was happy to oblige.

You never know exactly what's going to happen in a season, so it was quite adventurous of my publishers at Hodder Headline just to let me get on with it and see what occurred. There were certain inevitabilities: people would get sent off in controversial incidents; players would get bought and sold for phenomenal amounts of readies; Newcastle United would have a wonderful start to the season. There were other less likely possibilities: clubs might find themselves involved in the odd bit of scandal, if the previous season was anything to go by; mercurial geniuses, feted by the media, would suddenly stop scoring and everyone would wonder what all the fuss had been about; the Premier League would launch its own crisps (though Gary Lineker would still prefer to stick with another leading brand). Then there were things that were completely impossible: Graham Kelly would present *Top of the Pops*; an extra-terrestrial would sign for a Premiership club; Manchester United would lose 3–0 at home to Second Division opposition. I tried to press the managers involved on most of these matters and many more besides.

As a psychologist I have had the opportunity to work with football teams on a number of rewarding research projects involving such diverse areas as handedness and co-ordination and personality and motivation. In my experience, psychologists are not necessarily welcomed with open arms by everyone they work with (in a survey asking NASA astronauts what they hated most about their jobs, psychologists came second only to rectal thermometers) because they sometimes forget that, as well as studying the behaviour of human beings, they should themselves remember to behave like human beings. Not all of them do, but there is good and bad in every profession.

I found some of the tricks I'd picked up helped me to get the best out of the managers concerned, and to be honest, most didn't seem to mind what I was. It could have been much worse. I could have been a journalist.

As a fan, my record is perhaps a little shoddy, for while most fans who want to be respected remain loyal to a team until they die, my own loyalties have been described by one colleague as 'promiscuous'. At international level, I've always been a great fan of my native Czech Republic (or Czechoslovakia as was). Watching their penalty win over West Germany in the European Championships in 1976 on a flickering black-and-white set was one of my key formative experiences in growing up to love football. I've also always had a soft spot for Scotland, largely because of holidays there and the many friends I have from Caledonia. I can't hate the English team as much as I should, under the circumstances, but would be the first to say that, from my trips abroad following the team, Scottish supporters fully deserve their reputation as the best in the world – a laugh and a half and scarcely ever a fist flying.

At club level, it's even worse. My long-time support for Spurs evaporated when I decided to stop watching them play due to my dissatisfaction over how Alan Sugar had dealt with Terry Venables. While many Spurs fans drifted back over time, I was determined not to do so and instead decided to follow a team in a lower division, falling in with a group of friends who were regulars at St James' Park. No, it wasn't Exeter City. I wasn't *that* desperate.

No doubt as a result of my support, Newcastle United shot straight into the Premiership and have been there ever since. We celebrated my conversion to the ranks of the Toon Army with a ceremony which makes anything the Freemasons have so far invented seem dull by comparison.

Sometimes I lie awake at night worrying about this terrible change of allegiance, though I'm glad to say that Terry Venables has given it his blessing.

'People will say you're a turncoat supporter, and, of course, you are,' he pointed out. 'But people even change religion sometimes. It shouldn't be out of the question. If some individual comes to the club you love and behaves in a way that you find totally offensive and unforgivable, I think you should be allowed to start supporting another club . . .'

He did not elaborate further on the identity of such a hypothetical individual.

So that's it: I'm now an honorary Geordie (as well as an honorary Scot) and intend to remain so. The only problem was likely to be Euro '96. Who would I support? Scotland, the Czech Republic or a team managed by someone as sympathetic to my plight as Terry Venables? Ah, well. I could cross that bridge when I came to it. One thing seemed pretty certain: the likelihood of the Czechs meeting the Germans again in the final was one in a million.

Psychologists are supposed to be objective, and, when writing about football, that is going to be difficult. By the end of the book, my own irrational prejudices and quirks are likely to be readily apparent. But stick with it, gentle reader. Football is all about opinion. Mine may even occasionally be wrong.

Alfred Hitchcock once said that drama is life with the dull bits taken out. That's what football is to me. Unless you support Arsenal, in which case all the dull bits have been put back in.

1: Why Do I Do It?

'Smile first thing in the morning. Get it over with.'

W. C. Fields

If you're thinking about a career in football management, there's one thing you don't want to be, and that's a pessimist.

At times when everything seems to be stacked up against you, you've got to find something to be cheerful about. It's no good putting on that pained smile Graham Taylor always used to adopt, the grin seemingly held in place by cramming an inverted coathanger in the mouth, while the eyes betrayed the pain that lay beneath.

No, it's more than just putting a brave face on things – it's being able to smile in earnest that will see you through, a fact which became apparent to me one Saturday night in the middle of the season as I was having a drink and musing upon what distinguishes one football manager from another. That Wednesday, England had drawn nil–nil against Norway in the kind of match which made ninety minutes seem like several hours. Matches against Norway, the Arsenals of Europe, are seldom fun to watch and, to be fair, a draw against such a side is hardly a catastrophe, but the tabloids tend only to have two stories about the performance of a national team – either they are brilliant or they are disastrous, and on this occasion, England certainly weren't the former. Vilification of the manager was an inevitability. Most of the press pulled no punches. The result, coupled with press interest in manager (or 'Chief Coach') Terry Venables' pending court cases concerning various former business partners, most notorious among them Spurs chairman Alan Sugar, could definitely have been better. It's at times like these that managers must ask themselves whether the job is really worth it.

It had been a gloomy week all round, the rest of the papers largely crammed with details about murderess Rosemary West, who was about to be tried for her crimes.

'They tell me Rose West phoned Terry Venables this week,' boomed a voice across the room. 'It was to thank him for taking some of the heat off *her*!'

It was a line that could have been uttered in any pub across the country but, remarkably, it was spoken in Venables' own club, Scribes West, by his friend, England's chief scout, Ted Buxton. Sitting at his table at the back of the room, the manager laughed.

'How about a song from the Guv'nor now, eh?' continued the scout in his Saturday night role as karaoke compere. 'What'll you sing, Terry? How about "I Will Survive"?'

There was more laughter as Terry walked across the floor to the microphone. He seemed thoroughly relaxed, a man able to switch off from the pressures on this night as surely as if someone had pulled out the plug. It wasn't that he didn't care about the result. He knew he had work to do. But this was Saturday night, and no journalist was going to spoil that for him. You've gotta smile, and you've gotta know when to relax.

As the music swelled from the karaoke machine, it became clear that he had decided to give the suggested Gloria Gaynor hit a miss in favour of an older number, one of his own favourites.

'That Old Black Magic's got me in its spell . . . ,' he began.

It summed up the man. Sometimes behaviour can reveal as much to those interested in human nature as a conversation. Here was someone for whom a job, however important, wasn't something to make you sick with worry, something from which there was no respite. Yet, even in the words he sang, there were echoes of the life of a football manager:

'. . . So, Honey, down, up, down, up, down I go! Spinning around I go . . .'

I tried to imagine Graham Taylor doing the same thing. Somehow, I couldn't quite conjure up the image.

How do they keep going, these generals of the dressing room? How can they avoid ending up like Graham Taylor, battered, embittered, bowed? A sense of optimism, optimism that seems to fly in the face of the real picture, seems to help. Such optimism may be perceived as naive, but all optimism, by its very nature, falls into this category – otherwise it wouldn't be optimism at all, but realism.

Terry Venables has described himself as 'naive' and 'too trusting' in the past and, while this has probably hurt him in his business dealings, I feel certain it has helped him in his coaching. You have got to believe you can succeed. Never mind the statistics, never mind the world rankings, you've got to think that, all realistic considerations aside, you've got it in your power to do something special, to create that upset, to pull off a surprise.

Some managers like Glenn Hoddle and Tommy Burns (who features in this book) have their religious faith to keep them going, to provide that sense that victory is possible, even against the odds. Others can draw their faith from their trust in the people around them, the camaraderie and team spirit not only of players but also, more widely, friends, family, fans. The important thing seems to be to believe you can do it – win that Championship, that trophy, that cup – even if rational consideration suggests otherwise. After all, *someone has to win*, to quote a frequent justification for playing the lottery. And your odds of pulling off something spectacular in football are considerably higher than winning the jackpot.

I remember talking to an Irish fan about the bitter row that had arisen between former Ireland manager, Jack Charlton, and Irish sports journalist and ex-Millwall player, Eamon Dunphy. She told me: 'The thing is, fans like to *believe*. That's why they all loved Jack. Dunphy was always rational and realistic. No one wants that.' No one wants to be told that, realistically, their chances of success are extremely slim. They want to believe in the dream, they want to have faith. It is up to the manager to deliver that, game after game, in victory and, especially, in defeat. If he can do that, he knows he's doing well, and if he actually believes it himself, he's got it made.

The question remains: Why do they do it in the first place? Is it some unique form of masochism, this job where, when things are good, they are very, very good, but the minute that things begin to go wrong, you're as good as blindfolded, tied to a post and smoking your last cigarette, while the papers, the television and radio reporters (and often those who are supposed to be your fans) are baying for your blood – and, of course, your chairman, who is unlikely not to have noticed all the others, is a few feet away from you, toying with the trigger?

For an answer to this question, I decided to go to someone who was an old hand at the game. Jim Smith, presently at Derby, has had more ups and downs than a roller coaster at Blackpool Pleasure Beach. He was the first football manager I ever met, several years previously, when he was at QPR. There he was replaced by Trevor Francis, a disastrous appointment for the club. There was a massive clearout of players in what turned out to be a surprisingly heavy-handed managerial approach by Francis (most memorable was the notorious incident in which he fined Martin Allen for missing a match to attend the birth of his son, an episode which led to questions in the House).

On several other occasions, Smith left clubs to be followed by a manager who did a worse job. This was true at Portsmouth (now in the hands of Terry Fenwick, who was previously one of Smith's players at QPR) and Newcastle (where he was replaced by Ossie Ardiles, the purist but ineffectual manager loved by journalists, but generally the kiss of death to any side he comes to manage. Ardiles took the side to the brink of relegation before the new dawn that signalled the arrival of Kevin Keegan). He has also encountered some of the most notorious figures in the game, particularly Robert Maxwell, who was chairman of Oxford United, with whom Jim won the League Cup, only to leave for QPR immediately afterwards, when the two were unable to agree the terms of a new contract.

Smith told the papers that the stress of football management had had an adverse effect on his health, and when he left Portsmouth, many believed that he had left football management for good.

So why did he come back to manage Derby, where he had not been the chairman's first choice? What kept him at it?

His answer was both simple and honest: 'The mortgage.'

Well, you can't argue with that.

'The mortgage is at the end of it. At the start of it is the love of the game. Well, when I say "the game", it's no longer really a game, but a love of football. I find between seasons the worst time of the year when you're talking to players' agents about their contracts. But once pre-season training starts, and you're out there and you've got the banter and that camaraderie, it's just a special feeling.'

Another Smith ideally placed to give me an insight into the agony and ecstasy of it all is Alan Smith, a manager who has experienced most of the ups and downs in his time: the joy of promotion; the pain of relegation; an FA Cup final; coaching and managing at big clubs and small. While he may not have constant cause to look on the bright side of life, he retains a dry sense of humour, but has been through enough of the lows to know that if things can go wrong, they probably will. With independent business interests that have brought him financial success, why does he do it – and why does he feel others do the same?

> 'Managers want to remain involved in football, and I think most of the people in football probably know little else. If

they're successful at it, then, financially, it is of course *incredibly* rewarding. It's also rewarding in terms of what it does for your ego. Most managers are egoists to an extent – you can name some of the biggest egos, but I suppose we'd all be liars to say we're not. Either you're talking about someone who has been used to being in the public eye through having been a top player, or someone who sees it as a way of getting into the public eye, not having been a top player.

'I've found that when people drop out of it, they soon want to get back into it, despite all the psychological strain. I mean, if you think what Ian Branfoot went through while he was at Southampton, that must have been very hard. But he's gone straight back into it, and you could argue that he's going through it all again now at Fulham. As for Graham Taylor – look at what he had to put up with!

'Funnily enough, I don't think that I actually did it for any of those reasons, apart from the ego thing – I've got to say that there is that aspect to it. I just enjoyed football coaching and I think I genuinely believed that I could help make players slightly better. I've probably become a bit more cynical than that now. But there is a lot that goes with the job. You've probably heard me say this before, but the local football manager is usually better known than the local MP. I mean, if you were to ask who the MP is for Wolverhampton or for Lincoln, a lot of people wouldn't know, but a lot more may be able to tell you that Mark McGhee manages Wolves or that John Beck is the manager at Lincoln City. And there are quite a few people – not a lot, but quite a few – who may know that Alan Smith is the manager of Wycombe, but who wouldn't know the MP. So there's definitely that side to it.

'But there's no doubt at all that the Saturday is incredibly stressful, and if you're not doing well, it's even more stressful. Even so, there are a hell of a lot of perks in the job and I think managers sometimes don't realise this until they're not doing it, until they've got to go out and put petrol in their own car. A lot of them aren't very good businessmen and because they've always had a company car as a manager or a coach and because they've got used to going into a restaurant and not having to pay the bill, and somebody asking whether they'd like to play golf on Wednesday afternoon, it can come as a bit of a shock to the system when you find you're not doing that.'

At least you can still play golf on a Wednesday afternoon if you're between jobs.

'Well, you've got it with Phil Neal at the moment. I was reading an interview with him and he was saying that he is just fed up to the back teeth with golf. The job is also what you want to make it. If you don't want to put your heart and soul in it but you've got very good players and you can organise it that way, you can still have a reasonable lifestyle.'

This season, George Graham's enforced absence from management for a year, following his acceptance of a 'gift' from a Scandinavian agent, must have been immensely frustrating. He had done a lot of media work, but made no secret of his desire to get back to management as soon as possible.

'It's funny, but I always thought he was someone who had his life sorted out. I may be wrong, but I saw him admit it somewhere. He said somewhere that he didn't go and watch a lot of games, he didn't really drive himself. He took the training and he got all that organised, but he said he was able to detach himself from a lot of the grind of the job. He didn't spend half his time driving up the M40 or the M1, he just did his job and he seemed to have his lifestyle completely sorted out.'

But back to Alan Smith's own motivation. With the money from his property business, he surely didn't need the cash. (Indeed, it was claimed that, during his time as manager of Crystal Palace, his chairman played on this, the financial rewards offered having been unflattering to say the least, compared to other managers in his position.) So did he do it all for love, as the papers, somewhat romantically, suggested?

> 'I wouldn't really do anything for love too much, because I believe that if you earn money, it's almost a way you can judge your own worth. If you do a job, then some measure of how well you do it should come from what you can charge. A lot of people have said to me that I must do it for love, but I think that when Shirley Bassey does a concert, she doesn't do it for nothing. She charges for it. Frank Sinatra gets up and sings and he charges for it. We've just had Diana Ross come over for the rugby and she didn't do *that* for nothing. I'd say that is a bit of a misconception. So there's that to start with. Also, you've got to have a lotta lotta money to live for nothing. Even a house like mine [impressively large and comfortable, in a lightly populated part of the Surrey countryside] needs heating, lighting . . . there's an acre of garden at the back that needs cutting. If you live for another twenty years, your money may evaporate – I'm not saying that it would, but it may – after ten.
>
> 'Then again, you get a lot of people who say to me – Steve Coppell was one – that they hate football management and it interferes with what they want to do with their lives. But you cannot play golf eight hours a day, seven days a week. You've got to do something that gives you an edge. That's why these top financiers, Tiny Rowland and Forte and all that group of old buffers all got into the office at seven o'clock. Why do they do it? Maxwell! Why did he do what he did?'

It looks like we'll never know, in Maxwell's case. There was one chairman who wanted to manage the team if ever I saw one. But when it comes to what motivates football managers, evidently the love of the game is probably not the whole picture, but then neither are the perks and the pay packets.

What about the fame and recognition, enjoyable though it may be at times – can that contribute to the stress involved? Living your life and often making your mistakes in full view of the public must be difficult. I asked Mark McGhee about this pre-season at Leicester City.

> 'The problem is that the public treats footballers and football managers as public property, and almost as if they don't have feelings or families, don't have a wife and children, but are simply tools there to run a team. They feel we can cope and are impervious to hurt and therefore at times they treat us very badly. The compensation for that is that a successful football manager is well paid, and the conditions are good in that you are working in the open air most of the time. You're well looked after, so in that respect you're well compensated in many ways. But most of the people who are in the game, including those in management, are in it because they are *winners* and they demand that of themselves. They are therefore very vulnerable to the strain of losing because there are not that many teams who can win – there is only one team that wins the FA Cup and four teams that win a championship each year, so a very small number can really be completely successful. In a way, if someone wins the cup, all the others have failed and football managers, because of the sorts of people who go into football management in the first place, are especially vulnerable to the disappointment of having failed and the strain that it brings. I think it is the nature of the people who go into the job that makes them particularly vulnerable to the strain.'

As Alan Smith pointed out, if managers tend to have fairly large egos, then defeat must be particularly crushing, especially as it is so public.

'Yes, if you're very ambitious with quite a high ego, you are very vulnerable in defeat. It can really throw you.'

I wondered how difficult it was to switch off, and indeed, how much a manager even wanted to switch off. During the shorter and shorter summer breaks in the football season, do managers feel those same withdrawal symptoms fans sometimes get and long to get back to day-to-day involvement with the players and the club?

> 'It is something you miss. That's why we all do it. All club managers enjoy being part of that. That's why, when we go home at the weekend, we watch football matches on television, even after we've spent the whole week immersed in football. Every manager in the game ought to be like that, because they shouldn't be in it if they don't love it. I think you do have to be able to switch off at times, but mainly it's the only thing people think about. As a result, it isn't just an all-consuming passion for the manager himself, it's the same for his wife and family and everyone around.'

While the fans demand ambition of a manager, personal ambition may mean that he has his eye on a move to a bigger club. This was certainly true of Mark McGhee's stint at Leicester, which was to end halfway through the season, having lasted barely a year. His move there from Reading had annoyed fans at his previous club, and though his mid-season crossover to Wolverhampton Wanderers, ambitious in every sense of the word, was successful in terms of what he achieved, it left another set of angry fans in Leicester, feeling the usual sense of betrayal supporters experience when a star player or a successful manager disappears to ply his trade elsewhere. It is difficult in these situations for fans to step back from their emotional reactions and accept that a manager's career plans are pushing him beyond the club they love. A manager has to accept that this reaction will occur, of course, but the effects on his home life were something that Mark found particularly hard:

> 'We're all part of it. The families of managers end up involved. My boys were down there at school in Reading and they'd get confused by the differing opinions they'd hear all around them. At the club, the lads were concerned about whether they'd still be successful and were wondering why I'd left them and, of course, kids at school were saying Reading this and Reading that, so it can be very difficult for the families of managers.'

If Mark McGhee had thought that was bad, what the season had in store would result in serving up the same again, as he was to change clubs a second time in what was a very short interval.

All this was beginning to sound very depressing. It's certainly no picnic, but there has to be some optimism there. There has to be light at the end of the tunnel. To find out more, it was time to speak to one of the game's most famous optimists, a man whose spirit was so buoyant, you could use it as a lifeboat in the choppiest of waters.

2: The End of the Tunnel

'I'm frightened to stop, because there can be no life as enjoyable as this.'

Gordon Strachan

I first interviewed Dave Bassett in his office at Sheffield United's Bramall Lane ground, one of the managers who had let me come along to see him before the 1995-96 season had even begun. It was to be a turbulent season for him, but neither of us knew that at the time.

I don't think I'm alone among fans of other clubs in having the greatest respect for Dave, or 'Harry', as most people call him. Although he was one of the League's longest-serving managers at his present club, it was his achievements at his former club, Wimbledon, that were truly astonishing. The progress that this tiny side made from non-league football to what is now the top flight in nine seasons (in 1983, they topped the fourth division, by 1987, they finished sixth in the first division, now the Premier League) is well documented and broke all records. I wonder whether any other club will ever do it again, particularly in such a short space of time. Of course, not everyone was chuffed. There were those who believed that a poxy little side like Wimbledon had no right to be up there with what was considered the 'Big Five' in those pre-Jack Walker days (Manchester United, Liverpool, Everton, Spurs and . . . er . . . I forget the other one). Some of these people supported the 'sleeping giants', clubs that, like David Frost, must have done something good once, but you couldn't for the life of you remember what it was. Or when they did it. After all, ran the tired old argument, a club like, say, Blackpool has a fine tradition. Stanley Matthews and all that. OK, so they're rubbish *now*, but what about the glory days? Eh? Eh?

People who think along these lines have probably written a soul-searching, hand-wringing article for *When Saturday Comes*, or some such worthy publication for the older fan, going on about when their club was great. Some of them are obviously very old indeed if they can genuinely remember those days clearly. But Wimbledon? *Wimbledon?* Bloody philistines, the lot of them. Long-ball merchants. Kick-and-rush. So ran the orthodox version, anyway.

Nowadays, people's attitude to Wimbledon is changing. When they won the FA Cup in 1988, people began to stop and think. 'Surely they must have *something*?' they reasoned. They certainly do. What they appear to have (and if it's all an act, it deserves several Oscars!) is a near-perfect team spirit. I've witnessed it myself, and Harry and his successors, Bobby Gould and Joe Kinnear, can be duly proud of it. No one says that Wimbledon have the most technically gifted players in the country, but, by God, have they got a good atmosphere in the dressing room! And their players aren't that bad, either. Even the papers have begun to notice.

How did Dave Basset do it? That brings us to the question at the heart of this book: what is it that makes some football managers successful? What are the thoughts that go through their minds? What does it take? Can it be learned, or is being a good manager something you are born to do? After all, the pressure is enormous and yet Harry always seems to be smiling. As Sheffield United stared relegation in the face, he happily sent up his own 1993–94 close-season predicament on *Fantasy Football League*, making his entrance to the theme from *The Great Escape*, laughing and joking. If anyone deserves the title Eternal Optimist, it is Harry.

When asked about his approach, he was able to smile, even when talking about the painful bits . . .

> 'I don't think I think about the stress or what *might* happen. The stress is there because of the league table every week. There's always pressure and you're always looking to see if you're successful or unsuccessful. There doesn't seem to be an in-between spell. You're always associated with either success or failure. I think the reason a lot of people go into football management is because they are football fanatics; they've grown up with the game and football is a love, they enjoy it so much. You've got a love for it, a *desire* for it – love is probably the wrong word – and it's a desire that's insatiable. You become immersed in football, so you put up with all the stress.
>
> 'A lot of people couldn't cope with the pressure of being a manager. There are a lot of decisions to be made. You make decisions every week, like which team to pick or which tactics to teach. You have lots of decisions and a lot of people don't like making decisions. But you've no chance of becoming a football manager if you don't like making decisions.'

And, of course, you have to believe your decisions are the correct ones – which takes self-esteem and optimism. In fact, a combination of quick decision-making and an optimistic outlook has been shown by psychologists to be one of the best predictors of success in many jobs, particularly those involving the management of people – although few jobs entail the level of scrutiny that you have to accept as a football manager. Results are immediate and are tabulated from the off.

> 'There's a league table and after two games you're somewhere in there. You're near the top or near the bottom and

each week you've got an assessment of how you're doing – you can over-react to it! In other businesses, it's judged on the year. You can have three bad months and people just accept that it might be market forces or whatever, but the relevant data will tell you that the first three months might be a bit iffy and then you'll come strong. Football's like that as well. When I've been here at Sheffield United, in the Premier League, we had a couple of appalling starts and then came very strong in the second half of the season and finished in a different position, so you've got to look at it over the year. That's up to the board of directors, really. Sometimes the fans are screaming for your head and the media is doing the same and then managers battle, really. The screaming gets to a crescendo and then somebody has to pay for it and it's usually the manager.'

Harry isn't unrealistic, then. His optimism isn't one which exists in cloud-cuckoo-land. When he heard that fellow first division manager Mark McGhee had told me that he wasn't preparing for promotion this season, merely to consolidate, build his side and then aim for promotion the following season, he remarked, 'I wonder if his chairman sees it that way?' Somehow, Harry manages to look on the bright side within a realistic context:

'As a manager, I think you have to look at the job that you're doing with the club that you've got and you have to accept that club – what its potential is, what its position in the league is, its ability at that time, the people running it . . . Basically, the manager can only operate within the framework of what the directors have got. If the directors haven't got any money or they can't get the money in, and the club's not getting enough through sponsorship, kit and gate, you're probably going to struggle. You might find one gem but then you'll probably have to sell it – that's the situation. I know that here at Sheffield United we're a medium-sized club. We can't compete in buying big players and we're always vulnerable if somebody wants one of our players who is very good. We have to sell him, like we did with Brian Deane. *That is the situation.* We can't kid ourselves that we're Newcastle United or Manchester United. Some of our fans may dream and we all have a little dream, but in reality we can't do that. Sheffield United will only grow bigger by the board becoming more wealthy and deciding they're going down a certain road and expanding the club. I'm not just saying someone wealthy will come in and give millions to the manager. It might be coming in and developing the stadium in a different way, making sure there are more boxes, commercially exploiting it so you can bring in more money. The fact that you can bring in more money can eventually go back into building a team.'

Of course, in embarking on any money-making scheme, it is important not to annoy the Football Association's chiefs. Down in what used to be the Diadora League, Dulwich Hamlet had come up with a pre-season cracker. Those who live outside South London may have heard very little about Dulwich, but in their heyday they were one of the giants of the amateur game. Their stadium used to hold 20,000. Then for a time the club had no permanent home at all. Recently, a smaller, brand-new stadium was built on the site of the old one. To get back to their money-spinning idea: the lads had allowed a film crew into the club to shoot the boys working out at the gym, relaxing in the sauna and, inevitably, soaping themselves up in the showers to turn into a video for the lucrative new hen-night market. The result, *Dream Team – A Football Fantasy*, sold like hot cakes as soon as it hit the shops. However, as some of the shrewder players had guessed, the main market turned out not to be women celebrating hen nights at all – it shot straight into the gay video chart at stores like HMV and Virgin! No matter. The money was good and profits went straight back into the club. Not bad at all for half a day's work – and it evidently cheered up a few gay virgins into the bargain. Particularly enviable was the role in the first sequence to be filmed, in which one player was shown getting an unexpected massage from the extravaganza's squeaky-voiced female star, whose role was essentially to run about everywhere eyeing up the fellas. It was just as well he was lying on his front or the video might never have got a certificate.

All's fair in love and stripping off for the cameras, you might think, but not a bit of it! The FA felt that all this was 'bringing the game into disrepute', a catch-all offence which covers everything from removing your shirt after scoring a goal and spinning it around your head to making dozens of irregular payments to your players over a period of years. Naturally, if you have Alan Sugar's lawyers, offences like the latter can be overturned, but Dulwich Hamlet, despite having been picked by the production company because of their superb equipment (no pun intended), are literally not in the same league. Interestingly, they were hardly setting a precedent. Ian Walker, Ian Wright and the whole of Hendon FC had got their kits off for magazines the previous season, while Manchester United's packaging of Ryan Giggs and Lee Sharpe as sex objects to rival Take That (shirts off, plenty of manly sweat) can hardly go unnoticed. What had Dulwich Hamlet done wrong? They'd had a bit of a laugh, earned their club a bit of money and, if anything, promoted a bit of team spirit. You'd have thought the FA would have applauded their efforts!

Actually, for those who think this is marketing gone mad, a symptom of what the game has become in the cynical nineties, it must be remembered that Crystal Palace, 'The Team of the Eighties' did something very similar in the seventies, when manager Malcolm Allison invited sexpot Fiona Richmond to join the players in the team bath. (Famously, Allison claims that Terry Venables ran out of the bath so quickly that he thought he'd made a mistake about asking him to retire as a player!) It has even been said that he lost his job over that incident. You can't help wondering where people's sense of humour has gone sometimes.

Dulwich captain Russell Edwards, who works hand-in-glove with player-manager Frank Murphy, cares deeply about the fortunes of the club. As the side's 'Mr Fixit', he had organised things and dealt with the video company, thereby placing himself most obviously in the firing line. By coincidence, Russell had run in to Harry on holiday in the close season. The seen-it-all-before Sheffield United manager would no doubt have been amused by the club's predicament. Wimbledon had been through all that (at one point, famously, closing the season by mooning at the crowd). It all builds team spirit. Wimbledon's unpopularity with some fans of other clubs only helped to make that feeling of 'All for one and one for all' stronger. And then there were Harry's famous team-building stunts. Naturally, when he started at Sheffield United, those stunts came with him. Perhaps most memorable is the moment when he decided to take the words of Roy Wood and Wizzard ('I wish it could be Christmas every day') literally.

For a couple of seasons, Sheffield United had begun badly in the autumn, with early results suggesting to many that they were ripe for the drop. After Christmas, things traditionally improved and, come the end of the season, The Blades were triumphant survivors. Why not, in that case, celebrate Christmas in August *before the season began*? In 1992, that's just what Harry did:

> 'Yeah, that was a couple of seasons ago. I mean, we'd had a couple of seasons where we'd had a poor start and didn't start getting our game together and improving our results until after Christmas and we just thought it would be a laugh with the boys, a gimmick, to have a do before the season started with everyone going, and to call it a Christmas do. It did the trick – we beat Manchester United in the first game, but then we still ended up in the bottom little area and we still finished strong, so psychology with the players only plays a certain

amount. Sometimes it works and sometimes it doesn't. Sometimes you just try little ideas that you think will be something different, something that'll just stimulate things. And that's part of management, isn't it – stimulating them into enjoying what they're doing and getting results.'

Dressing up as Father Christmas and dispensing presents to the lads – what a guv'nor! I couldn't help feeling that Harry is one manager I wouldn't mind playing for. Ron Atkinson is another manager who has a reputation for taking his players along for a karaoke night or some other event to pump up the camaraderie a bit. I asked Harry if he could see a similarity between Ron's style of management and his own.

'Every manager is different, and I certainly wouldn't say that what I do or what Ron Atkinson does is right or that somebody else is wrong in what they do. Everyone has their own management style and, to be quite honest, I couldn't care less about what everyone else does. I'm not really interested. I'm only interested in what is right for me and what I think is right for my club and my players. I mean, we might go go-karting for the day and have racing and do something different. We've done paintballing. We've gone off with the army and done some assault courses, army training in tents and everything else. I just think it's something a bit different to get the players going. Some people might think, "I don't fancy that idea", so you might have a break instead, going away for a few days, maybe having a day at the races or a night out in a Chinese restaurant. All these things sometimes have to be done, but not on a regular basis – only when you feel it's the right time and that again is down to the judgement of the manager. You can have a drink and a good laugh and the players feel relaxed. You want to make them feel relaxed, but at the same time for them to know that they have got an important job. They have to get results and, whilst you can have a good laugh, there is a serious side to it as well. As long as the management are aware of that, the players also become aware of it. What happens sometimes is that everybody becomes a little more tense and it can be counterproductive. The art is in making it look easy – whatever you're doing. If you can make management look easy and playing look easy, then you know you've got it. It sounds simple to say, but it's not easy to produce that situation.'

Harry's spirit seems to have survived at Wimbledon. Joe Kinnear has kept the torch burning and fills Harry's shoes superbly. Bigger clubs scratch their heads and wonder what a club like Wimbledon, whose attendances in thousands can be counted on one hand, does to achieve such warmth and solidarity between the players. Joe revealed to me that when a player leaves Wimbledon, there is never any acrimony – and they are always welcome back to visit the lads. Indeed, he accepts that Wimbledon, because of their size, will always be a selling club. In recent seasons they have lost many of their best players to other clubs and others are continually rumoured to be on the way. Well, *lost* is hardly the word. They've made a mint out of them, money that is much appreciated, given the club's low gate receipts. The club's state-of-the-art training facilities, including a fine club house, were purchased through the sale of the players.

One of them, however, couldn't bear to stay away. Vinnie Jones, a product of the Dave Bassett league-climbing side and king of team spirit, a player who embodies everything that Harry and Joe's tradition represents (and we mustn't forget Bobby Gould, at the helm for the club's historic FA Cup win over Liverpool in 1988, who, just as the season got going, accepted the challenge of managing Wales), is back at the club, almost certainly for the rest of his playing career. Having played the wild rover for a couple of years, linking up with Harry at Sheffield United, following a spell at Leeds, and then going via Chelsea back to the club where his heart lay, this was one return of the prodigal to set Great Uncle Bulgaria and his Wombles dancing round the Common. In his autobiography, *A Kick in the Grass*, Vinnie describes the tears he shed when he first left Wimbledon. Leaving a place with such team spirit can make the hardest of hard men cry (and if we had any doubt that he was hard, we had only to look at his video, *Soccer's Hard Men*).

In fact, it seemed that the previous season had never stopped. So much transfer dealing took place over the summer, leading to so much news coverage, that those who don't follow football must have thought matches were still going on. Dutch internationals Dennis Bergkamp and Ruud Gullit signed for Arsenal and Chelsea respectively, while Paul Gascoigne made the move from Italy back to Britain, although, to the surprise of many, he chose Scotland over England and went to Rangers. I met him briefly while I was on my summer holiday in Loch Lomond, one of the most picturesque parts of the British Isles, and he was looking slim, fit and ready for anything.

Not everyone was enjoying the close season, though. At Manchester United, three of the club's most valued players jumped ship, Mark Hughes to Chelsea, Paul Ince to Inter and Andrei Kanchelskis (eventually) to Everton. This had followed a season where The Red Devils, tipped by everyone (including Vinnie Jones) to win everything when the season began in 1994, instead won nothing (not that they would be down for long, as things were to turn out). The fans were gutted.

Harry, however, had been through worse – much, much worse. At the end of the 1993–94 season, shortly after his defiant appearance on *Fantasy Football League*, Sheffield United faced Chelsea in the final match of the season. A Mark Stein goal in the ninetieth minute – *the final minute of the season! The last kick of the game!* – saw Sheffield United relegated. The effect on morale was devastating, as Harry admitted when he forced himself to look back on that day.

> 'It's hard. That knocked me sideways. It was my biggest disappointment ever. Had we gone to Chelsea knowing that we had to win to stay up and we hadn't achieved it, it would have been different. We'd have been relegated and we'd have been disappointed, but we would have had a different view on it. When all of a sudden you're up, you're winning, then you're drawing, then you're winning, then you're drawing and it looks like it's going to be a draw and you know you're up and then *that* happens in the last moment . . . it's cruel. Football is cruel, life's cruel in a lot of ways. Things happen. I mean, people have been far worse off, with injuries and so on, but it was a psychological and an emotional thing and it takes a long time to recover. I don't think you ever recover from it. It'll always be there in the back of your mind, below the surface, like a storm cloud. There's a big storm and then gradually the clouds drift away, but then you get more clouds. It affected me and I'm sure it affected the players. It affected a lot of people . . . our fans . . . To be honest, last year the club was in a limbo state, there was a sort of strangeness about it, a numbness. The whole season was affected by that result at the end of the previous season. I think we've got it out of our system now and that we shall see more reality in the coming season. There was perhaps a feeling that we'd been dealt such a cruel blow that we'd get straight back into the Premier League, that it was our divine right. But that wasn't the case.'

To make things worse, the relegation had also hinged on another match between Everton and Harry's old club, Wimbledon. Everton's victory, which kept them up, was largely due to some dreadful goalkeeping by Wimbledon's Hans Segers. It was then alleged that Segers, along with John Fashanu and Bruce Grobbelaar, had conspired to throw matches for money. Initially most people found the idea laughable, but the police thought otherwise. Joe Kinnear insisted that he believed Segers to be innocent and would feel extremely disappointed and betrayed if he was found to be guilty. Harry felt similarly:

> 'Well, you can never prove these things and if someone did prove it in due course, well, that's not for us to deal with. That's life. It would be sad if that was the case. But you can't get involved with rumour.'

Sheffield United had the worst start of the season you could imagine. They lost their first five games and found themselves at the very bottom of the first division. In an atmosphere of boardroom uncertainty, with chairman Reg Brealey's rule looking increasingly shaky and a quarter of the stadium not built, it is hardly surprising that player confidence was not sky high. Poor starts were nothing new to Harry, though. Sheffield United had had more of these than the Grand National. What did he do when the going got tough?

> 'Obviously the players and the manager have low morale. When the club's going through a bad patch, it's not easy to keep yourself bouncing along, pretending nothing's wrong and everything in the garden's rosy. It's not! Everybody's aware of the situation. I mean, you can't become morose and you can't become completely bloody mad. You've got to try and temper that with realism, knowing what's required and keeping a fairly good ship, but at the same time, everyone's aware of the importance of it. In the objectives and goals you're aiming for, if you've got a bit behind, you've got to start redefining your goals and where you're going.'

Don't write them off just yet, I thought to myself. These things pass. Already there were rumours that Texas Homecare supremo Mike McDonald would take over from the previous regime to bring some much-needed stability to the club. The Blades might not have got off to Wimbledon's flying start, but these were early days. For the club, and for Harry, too, things were set to get better – though not in the way I imagined at the time.

Whatever happened, I was sure at the start of the season that Harry's optimism and his sense of humour would never desert him. Sometimes in football they're all you've got to keep you sane.

You've got to laugh. And it helps if you still believe in Santa Claus.

3: Early Doors

'Que sera sera. *Whatever will be will be . . .*'

Doris Day

Or, as the more recent variant has it, 'Tell me Ma, me Ma, I won't be home for tea, we're going to Wem-ber-lee, tell me Ma, me Ma'. Ah, yes! At the beginning of the season, anything is possible. Five losses on the trot may dash the hopes of a lesser manager than Harry Bassett, or send shivers up the spine of a squeamish and short-termist chairman, but for others, the early part of the season was looking altogether brighter.

It seemed a good idea to check out managers' concerns early on in the season and see how they were planning for the coming months. In some cases, their words were set to come back and haunt them . . .

In Leicester, they were laughing. Leicester City, having been the worst club in the Premier League the previous season, were riding high on top of the First Division. It was already being whispered around Filbert Street that they were set to go straight back up, back to the lovely, lucrative Premiership.

To get into the Premier League is more important than ever for First Division sides nowadays. It's no longer simply a question of getting more fans through the turnstiles if a club is doing well. More significantly, the payout from Sky for televising Premiership matches is enormous. There is also the money from merchandising, already substantial at a well-supported club like Leicester, but likely to increase with Premier League status, armchair fans being more willing to shell out the readies for some replica kit or nick-nack if they've seen the side on the telly. Big clubs like Manchester United now make considerably less than half their revenue from gate receipts.

Unlike many fans, I don't think this is a terrible thing. True, it is hard on supporters' pockets. Taking the family out to a match can be very expensive indeed, particularly if a Premiership side is involved. But you have to pay through the nose for *everything* nowadays: Alton Towers; the pictures; a rock concert . . . even museums and galleries charge a fortune. That's free enterprise for you. For all that, football in all its weird and wonderful guises is more popular now than ever before and if it means that kids today wander around the streets of Kingston-upon-Thames with Man United shirts on, then I can bite my lip and let them. As a Newcastle United fan, I know that all this is just another symptom of a so-called disease in the game which has produced a brand-new stadium and a host of exciting and expensive players at my club. If disease it be, I've happily caught it. Those who hanker for yesterday when players were treated like cattle and liking football was considered akin to mental illness (liking Arsenal continues to be seen in this way) can go and whinge about it somewhere else (on Sky TV, in Phil Thompson's case).

But I digress. Was Leicester City's new manager, Mark McGhee (one of the best penalty-takers Newcastle ever had!), who had taken the job the previous season knowing that Leicester were doomed to relegation, relishing the possibility of taking them straight back up again? Funnily enough, when I spoke to him pre-season, he was playing a very cautious game:

> 'Obviously, that's the target. We have to look at where our chances stand at the moment in that respect and what we have

to do to improve our chances. There is a bit of work to be done but we have come down not as a Premier Division side who have been unlucky, but as a team that's proven not to be nearly good enough for the Premier League. So we are building for the following season, when we envisage being back in the Premier League, so when we arrive there we've got a better team. That team should be good enough to get us out of the First Division, of course, but that's what we're looking at – we're looking ahead and not just, in the short term, at getting out of the division.'

Talking to *Matchday*, the Official Magazine of the Endsleigh Insurance League, he was markedly less reserved: 'Quality is going to be the key word at this club from now on. We're heading back to the Premier League and we're going to be doing it in style . . . Our objective, right from the word go, has been to get a top place in the First Division and automatic promotion this season. If we can't get into the top two, then it has to be the top six and win promotion to the play-offs. But I think we're on the right track for a swift return to the Premiership.'

I suppose you have to turn on that kind of enthusiasm, knowing the fans will be reading the magazine, which is published monthly. Aware that this book would appear at the end of the season to come, Mark was showing a little more caution when he spoke to me. It also suggests that it is important what the players read. You have got to be as optimistic as possible for them and the fans.

McGhee had been forced to sell the club's star player, Mark Draper, to Aston Villa, now managed by Brian Little, the manager he had replaced at the club and now not a popular chappie with the Leicester supporters. Hell hath no fury like fans scorned. Equally upset had been certain Reading supporters when Mark left the club where he had cut his managerial teeth to go to big-time Leicester.

'There is a lot at stake for me because people have been asking me about my decision to come here and whether it was the right decision,' he said before the play-offs which gave his old club the possibility of promotion into the Premiership. 'Especially as, by the time the book comes out, Reading could have been up and back down again! The answer I give people is: ask me in a year's time. In a year's time look at the situation I'm in and look at the situation that Reading's in and then judge if I've made the right decision or not. I think I'll be proven to have made the right decision. So it's a big, big season for me in that respect. I have got a lot of people to prove wrong. I don't think anybody has yet doubted my ability, but they've doubted my decision. I'm determined to prove to people that I made the right decision.'

Well, Reading didn't go up and back down again. They didn't go up in the first place. At Wembley, they couldn't turn on the magic and remained in the First Division, where Leicester now sat. Whether Mark breathed a secret sigh of relief is known only to him. What he did reveal, though, was that his move to Leicester was very much part of a long-term plan:

> 'I think that I have quite a clear picture of my career. I believe that I started not at the bottom, because Reading was a Second Division team, but fairly well down the pecking order. I felt, the day I started, that I was on a ladder and that if ever I was going to be the manager of one of the top half-a-dozen clubs in the country, then I was going to have to move up that ladder gradually. I saw Leicester as a sort of intermediate step, before a big step. I think that I want one day to manage, if possible, the biggest club in the country, whichever it would be at the time. In order to achieve that, I have to be successful here, so that's why I'm here. It's not just about being promoted in the coming season, because I believe you can fail to win promotion but fail well, as Wolves have done. I mean, Wolves are a good team. They've had a lot of injuries and they've come very close. He deserves credit for what he's done. Probably, next season they'll be promoted.'

By 'he', Mark meant Wolves and former England boss, Graham Taylor. Unsuccessful and unloved at national level, he had returned to club football with some success, but not enough to clinch promotion. As the new season started, however, it was Mark McGhee at the top of the tree and Taylor's Wolves far below, the tabloids running the usual rumours that the axe was about to fall. Mark's path to the very top was looking clearly signposted.

What was to follow at Leicester and at Wolves would no doubt make interesting viewing.

Meanwhile, one manager was already at the very top. Rangers are the biggest club in Britain. Yes, Man United are up there somewhere as well, but I think Rangers have probably got the edge. Mark McGhee might not be aiming for the top job there, given that he used to play for arch-rivals Celtic (though after the Mo Johnston transfer sensation, anything is now possible), but the present incumbent has one of the most enviable jobs in the game. His name is Walter Smith. And he had just bought Gazza.

Paul Gascoigne's move to Scotland surprised many people, not least the newspaper journalists who had been busy linking him with just about every club in the country in their usual unconvincing pretence that they know what's going on. Many within the game thought he would go to Middlesbrough, newly promoted to the Premiership, linking up with young manager Bryan Robson for whom Gazza has a lot of respect. Middlesbrough is very close to Newcastle, where Paul's parents live, and, if you can overlook the huge ICI factory and a cock a deaf ear at opposing fans singing 'Hey, Boro – leave your kids alone!', you can probably enjoy quite a comfortable life there.

But Paul went to Rangers, settling on the bonnie, bonnie banks of Loch Lomond, an idyllic place where he could fish to his heart's content. Was it just a case of take the money and run?

'When a player has reached the top end of his career, it's very much a case of *where he wants to go*,' Walter pointed out. 'Financial aspects of the deal are less crucial. The bigger clubs in Britain will all be able to satisfy those. So he'll come to a club, looking at it from outside, see how it's projected over a particular period and make his choice.'

If I remember the *Dandy* correctly, though, the Jocks and the Geordies were always fighting one another. What could make a player so proud of his Tyneside roots want to settle in Scotland, playing for a Glasgow club?

> 'I think one thing he looked at was that we have a reputation for being a really good club, that's the main thing. We've had a lot of good players here now that have played at big clubs, like Ray Wilkins and people like that. They've always spoken very highly of Rangers and I think that's helped us a great deal in this context, a lot of English players having played here. Brian Laudrup, for example, had heard through a number of people about the fact that we play well and that it was an enjoyable place to come. The players must *enjoy* working and coming here. We've got full gates for every home game. He's playing up front in a lovely stadium, so if he's got ability, that's where he wants to show it. So that part is already supplied by Rangers. But there are other things as well. There's Scotland and the people of Scotland. A lot of English players coming up here have really loved being in Scotland and have stayed up here. I think Paul Gascoigne had also picked up from talking to players that ours is a good dressing-room atmosphere and it's a very happy place to come and play. I think when a new player comes into a club, he appreciates the camaraderie.'

And with the likes of Coisty, Durranty and the rest, Rangers' reputation goes before them. Even if Hateley, one player fortunate enough to have been born with a surname already ending in 'y', ran off to join those other Rangers, QPR, early on in the season, it was still a squad noted for its 'characters'. Walter revealed that one team-building device the club uses is the infamous 'Rangers Lunch', where the team hole themselves up in a restaurant, start off at midday and are still going at midnight! The only problem with these lunches is squeezing them into an already packed and tiring fixture list.

So, dressing-room bonhomie and the superior fishing opportunities that exist in Scotland seem to have been instrumental in luring Paul Gascoigne to Rangers, ahead of the other clubs who could have paid the same money. As the season progressed, the club's fans would grow to appreciate just how valuable the pull of the Rangers Lunch and the availability of salmon in Loch Lomond were to be.

One thing which Walter Smith finds has made his job a million times easier is the fact that, in the case of Rangers, the full support of his chairman really does mean the full support of his chairman and is not a euphemism for 'start looking around, you'll be out of here by Tuesday'.

Having secured his prize buy, then, the trick was going to be remaining at the top. Arch-rivals Celtic were assembling a formidable side under young manager Tommy Burns.

> 'It's always a problem, being right at the top of the League every season. People just expect you to be there, and if you slip up, they're not going to forgive you. Our big challenges this season are maintaining our position in domestic competition, but also doing better in Europe than we did last year. We know that Celtic are going to be mounting more of a challenge and the European Cup, or Champions League, is our chance to prove ourselves on a bigger stage.'

Again, it would be interesting to watch.

It's quite a step from the enormity of Rangers to the tininess of Wimbledon, who have regularly shamed some of the biggest sides in the country without even owning their own ground. But pre-season Wimbledon was a happy club. The side with the worst attendances in the Premiership (and, according to an interesting survey early on in the season, the poshest fans – June Whitfield is one such) have a reputation for being totally bonkers. Never mind your Rangers Lunches – how about sending the players off for a spot of ballet training or a trip to the Raymond Revuebar? This nuttiness has served the club well. Since their meteoric rise to the top, they have never gone down, generally finishing each season in the Premiership's top ten.

If they could escape the drop this season, despite having to sell key defender Warren Barton (though the five million they got for him from Newcastle wasn't a bad price at all), it would represent a decade in the top flight. Early on in the season, a mass shaving of heads, leaving all the players looking like Vinnie Jones, was the first step in generating the empathy and sense of collectivism that you need to survive when the odds are against you. Come the end of May, if things have gone well, it shouldn't just be the barber who's smiling.

Presiding over the side created by Sam Hammam's investment and, increasingly, by the sale of player after player to bigger clubs with considerably bigger wallets, is manager Joe Kinnear.

Joe, like Dave Bassett before him, is a larger-than-life, intensely down-to-earth optimist. His ansafone message informs you that unless you're the chairman of Real Madrid, Barcelona or AC Milan, you're going to have to wait.

> 'I think I'm successful mainly because of my personality and the way I approach things. I *love* it. I enjoy it. I look forward to it. It's the passion and the love of the job that keep me going. If there's one criticism, it's that I spend far too much time on football and possibly not enough time with my family, but I believe that if you're going to do it right, you've got to be in it two hundred per cent. I could spent twenty-four hours a day of

every single day enjoying it. I enjoy buying players, spotting players, bringing them in, producing them and then selling them on at a profit.'

While Jim Smith has said that the pre-season transfer ritual and maze of contract negotiations is, for him, the worst part of the job, Joe Kinnear positively relishes it.

'Every decision to buy I make myself. I have my own private hit list, and update it through all my scouts. I have about twenty-five players in every position and I rate them and grade them accordingly. So I've got that at my fingertips. I know what type of player I'm looking for. I understand the position I'm in. I'm in a difficult position in that I'm possibly the only manager in the Premier League without finances. Even a club like Crystal Palace has far in excess of what I have. We average about nine thousand, which is nowhere near enough for our budgets, so therefore we've got to have spending codes and wage codes and look at players who I believe will be future stars. We've had a tremendous record. I don't believe there is anybody in football who could match it. Since I've been here, I've sold Keith Curle for 2.7 million, Terry Phelan for 2.4 million, Dennis Wise for 1.7 million, John Scales for 3.7 million, John Fashanu for 1.5 million, and I've just sold Warren Barton for 5 million. We've broken records, particularly with defenders. We've sold the most expensive full-back ever. It's sad in some respects, watching them go, because we go to great lengths to look after the players here.'

And what of the agents, who will no doubt be keeping percentages of the figures quoted for themselves? Is it true that they deliberately unsettle players at clubs, encouraging them to move elsewhere so that they can pocket their cut of the transfer fee? Walter Smith and David Murray would have had to deal with Mel Stein and Len

Lazarus, the solicitor and accountant who act as Paul Gascoigne's agents. Joe will have dealt with, among others, the showbiz-loving, cigar-chomping Eric Hall, agent to Dennis Wise, John Scales and others. And there are many, many more.

> 'Agents unsettling players? We've probably had three or four cases of that. I mean, the more valuable a player is, the more he becomes surrounded by numerous agents. Now that the FA have tidied it up with agents having to lodge a hundred grand with the FA, the dodgier ones are being weeded out, which I think is a good thing. Agents have got a role to play, and provided they play it straight and honest, there's nothing wrong with it. It'll be interesting to see what happens, because now, if they haven't got the FA licence, you can't deal with them – we have to deal with registered agents. The Premier League Agents' Charter. Rules are rules.'

And so began a new season. For the first few matches, Wimbledon topped the Premiership, Leicester were on the top spot in the First Division and Rangers were number one in Scotland. But these were early days. A lot could change . . .

And what of Dulwich Hamlet, the video stars? They had a blinding start to the season as well in both the ICIS League and the qualifying rounds of the FA Cup. A 7–1 victory over Southwick in the first qualifying round was achieved without a single hat trick. Player-manager Frank Murphy was chuffed: 'It shows that we play as a team,' he pointed out. He is the first to give credit to his players, including the side's deadly strikeforce of Willie Lillington and Paul Whitmarsh, the mere mention of whom should earn me a drink, and to his assistant Johnny Johnson.

Teamwork was the key to the non-league side's early success. A combination of more experienced players, many of whom were once with league sides, and younger footballers who learn from them has led to a real sense of team cohesion. While Rangers may have their famous lunches, it is Dulwich's coach trips that are legendary for their sheer spontaneous hilarity – the further afield, the better. The club's most dedicated jokers and drinkers sit at the back (christened 'Black Hats'), the middle of the coach accommodates the 'Grey Hats' (generally 'Black Hats' who are knocking on a bit and have wives and kids and such things, or younger players who have yet to be initiated into this crucial part of the club's culture) and the 'White Hats' (boring) sit at the front. Antics the like of which would probably be frowned upon by league clubs – certainly those in the Premiership – go unchecked and very good for team spirit it is, too.

That's not to say that the club doesn't take the game seriously. The training requires rigorous discipline and can be very intensive. Nevertheless, it's very much a work-hard-play-hard philosophy at the club, and in a game where playing *is* working, they relax pretty hard as well! Many Premiership players would probably forfeit a proportion of their ridiculous salaries to be able to enjoy the relative anonymity and sheer hell-for-leather camaraderie that can flourish in a good non-league side.

Perhaps everything is different at this level. Certainly, the role of the manager is less apparent here. (At least, it *seems* less apparent when things are going well. If things start to crumble, his role becomes more noticeable, as I soon discovered!) Everyone *does* pull together and if other clubs envy the team spirit at Wimbledon, well, perhaps even Wimbledon might envy a side like Dulwich. If the former are The Crazy Gang, Dulwich Hamlet are one hundred per cent certifiable! Fortunately for them, if anyone is too far off their trolley, the Institute of Psychiatry is just round the corner from the club's Champion Hill stadium.

4: Psycho, Psycho

'You may be right. I may be crazy.
But it just might be a lu-na-tic you're looking for . . .'

Billy Joel

Of course, when I said that Dulwich Hamlet were certifiable, what I meant was nutty in a nice kind of way. The way Scotland supporters are when they go abroad. Pissed, singing, dancing, mooning but above all friendly with it. Unthreatening. A good laugh. The acceptable face of lunacy, like Marty Feldman or Madness singing *House of Fun*.

Then again there is a different kind of nutter in football – the kind who stamps on your neck, scrunches your scrotum and elbows you repeatedly in the face; the kind who delights in being called 'Psycho' by his team-mates; the kind who, in a different era, would have been a Viking or a Hun (no disrespect to Rangers players intended) or a Visigoth.

Before we condemn these men too loudly, though, it is important to bear certain facts in mind.

Firstly, there is nothing new about them. Indeed, hard men from the past reckon that today's game has gone soft. Several broken limbs per week were part and parcel of the good old days.

Secondly, these men are generally revered by their fans, considered natural leaders and superb motivators both on and off the field by their clubs and are generally among a side's more indispensable assets.

Thirdly, most of these people are actually really nice men off the field. Canny blokes. Top lads. Diamond geezers. Female journalists from football magazines go and interview them, looking for the big softie at the heart of the beast, and seldom walk away disappointed. They don't have far to look. Like a driver foaming at the mouth with 'road rage' who gets home and, a couple of drinks later, is the nicest person you've met, so these players, when they get away from the ground (you'll note I haven't said 'get off the pitch', because it takes a while to wind down – there have been incidents in tunnels that would make the most experienced staff of London Underground wince) can be, yes, all right . . . rather lovable. It is only through the hazy glow of nostalgia that this is sometimes recognised. How everyone respects Nobby Stiles nowadays, yet what a little thug he was, if we're going to be objective about it!

Probably the most notorious hard man I got to know a little is Mark Dennis. He was the tabloids' answer to Freddy Krueger a few years ago, much in the way that a player like Julian Dicks fills this role now. Indeed, Dicks has said in interviews that Dennis was something of an inspiration to him. They were at Birmingham City together (a team which, later in the season, had several players involved in one of those unsavoury tunnel incidents I mentioned earlier). Off the pitch, however, Mark Dennis was one of the most likeable players I have met. At the time, as a young psychology researcher still learning the ropes, I found it hard to reconcile the warm, welcoming persona with the fact that his red cards were well into double figures, awarded on a couple of occasions after the match had finished for what happened on the way back to the showers!

Everyone knew that Mark had his problems off the pitch. There was a messy divorce involving a dispute over the custody of his daughter, a court case involving sex with a teenager (he got off), getting knifed while waiting for a taxi after a PFA dinner and, as he has since admitted in the papers, a strong dependency on cocaine. None of this, however, got in the way of what an agreeable person he was. There was the other side of him: QPR's PFA representative; the volunteer who stayed behind after training to help his younger team-mates; the player who manager Jim Smith looked upon almost as a son and one of the best left backs never to have played for England (in fact, those who wear the Number 3 shirt are unusually well represented in the Football Psychos Hall of Fame).

I asked Jim Smith if there was anything a manager could do to channel such aggression into something positive. Did he have any little hints he could pass on to others?

> 'To be honest, all you can do is talk and preach and talk and preach. You try to get a player like that to control the worst excesses of their temper, but there are no magic tricks. It is very, *very* hard. One thing you find in football, perhaps more than in other areas, is that it's very hard to get a leopard to change his spots. We all like to *think* we can do it, but it's extremely rare that we really can. You might be able to change them for a little while, but players revert back to type. When they are younger, like Mark Dennis was when I was first his manager, it's a little bit easier than when they're more mature . . .'

If 'mature' is the right word here!

> '. . . I've never been one for fining players unless they've been really stupid, because I think that's a negative approach, but you just have to keep talking to them. What you try to stress is that it's all very well them getting punished and booked, but what they have to think about is the damage it does to the team as a whole, and perhaps the entire club. A club can get a reputation on the strength of one or two

aggressive players. You have to keep reminding them that the club is the important thing, and they owe it to the club, because that's who's paying their wages, that they stay and play as many games as possible in one year.'

As the season began to get going, football's hard men dominated the headlines. West Ham's Julian Dicks was shown on camera to be stamping on Chelsea player John Spencer's head. Had the match not been live on Sky Sports, nothing would have happened. John Spencer himself, keen to show he was no big girl's blouse, brushed off the incident saying that these things happen in the game. (Though it must be said that anyone who chooses Pollok in Glasgow as his favourite holiday resort must see life from a somewhat unusual perspective. Not that I can talk. I've actually been on holiday to Pollok myself. But that's a different book.) The FA took the incident further, however, and ended up suspending Dicks, giving him the equivalent of a late red card. Meanwhile, Julian's daughters got bullied at school over the incident. That'll be violence leading to more violence, I shouldn't wonder.

Vinnie Jones, meanwhile, got the other side of the coin. Initially sent off for apparently head-butting Liverpool's Stan Collymore (along with a team-mate who, after a delay, was then confusingly allowed back on), he was cleared by the FA when video evidence showed that he didn't do it. His red card was reduced to a booking, though the Scousers who run my local reckon he still gave him an uppercut. I suspect a few Nottingham Forest fans quite enjoyed all this.

One person who paid dearly for an unmistakable head-butt was Everton's Duncan Ferguson, nicknamed 'Duncan Disorderly' by the tabloids. His history makes that of Mark Dennis read like an account of the works of St Francis of Assisi. The incident happened while he was at Rangers, was captured on camera and reached its conclusion with Duncan being sent to Barlinnie, the Glasgow jail that has Jimmy Boyle as its most famous graduate (it taught him to give up the life of a violent moneylender – the big bucks were in writing best-sellers). This was the first time as far as anyone can remember that a player was sent to jail for an incident that happened during the game. It had nearly happened some years back when Celtic and Rangers clashed, but they all got off with fines, and the Cantona incident the previous season had been just off the pitch. Anyway, he ended up not going to jail after all in the end because he's French, a genius, et cetera. Duncan ended up serving six weeks of his sentence, after which he was released to a hero's welcome from the blue half of Merseyside.

It is significant that in all of these incidents, just as in the Rodney King police brutality trial in the States, the presence of cameras was vital. We probably don't realise half of what went on in the past because film has not preserved it for posterity. Nowadays, when just about everything has been filmed, often from umpteen different angles, the evidence is there for all to see. Was it really a more gentlemanly game in years gone by? I very much doubt it.

What do managers make of it all? I asked Dave Bassett, whose sides have always been tagged with the label that they play intensely competitive and indeed aggressive football, and who has managed Vinnie Jones at Wimbledon and at Sheffield United, whether certain players find it difficult to separate being committed and competitive from being physically aggressive, as some of the research I had done with my colleague Stephen Smith suggests.

> 'People relate competitiveness to aggression and physical intimidation, but being competitive just means you want to beat somebody. Running for that ball . . . Can I get there before you? Winning that header, getting up there. That's competitive, too. It isn't just about kicking. Being competitive is also about anticipating things. Can you read what's going to happen? Are you clever? Can you outwit the guy that you're marking or who's marking you?
>
> 'People like to pigeon-hole things and when they talk about

being competitive, they talk about Vinnie Jones. They don't talk about other players. They don't talk about Matt Le Tissier. Matt Le Tissier is competitive, too. He's competitive in his free kicks and corners – he takes marvellous free kicks. Vinnie can't take a free kick to save his life. So if you said to Matt Le Tissier: Who's going to win the tackle? Vinnie Jones. Who's better in the air? Vinnie Jones. But who's going to take a good free kick, a brilliant corner? Matt Le Tissier. So Vinnie wins two and Matt wins two.'

Indeed, by mid-October, the tabloid caricatures of Jones the thug and Le Tissier the unsung genius were crumbling. When Wimbledon lost their keeper against Newcastle at St James Park, Vinnie stepped into the breach to rapturous applause from the Geordie fans. He gave a theatrical bow and then proceeded to let in lots of goals, but he had won the hearts of the opposing fans, as had Dennis Wise a few weeks beforehand. Halloween might have been just round the corner, but Vinnie was no longer someone to be scared of. The following day, Matt Le Tissier got sent off (the first Southampton player to take the long walk in what seemed like aeons) against Liverpool. It was for a second yellow card, but the two crunching late tackles concerned would easily have earned him a transfer from his own *Unbelievable* video to Vinnie's *Soccer's Hard Men* video.

And what about that bit in Vinnie's video in which he said that a player like Gary Lineker, who had never been so much as booked, couldn't be playing with much heart, much commitment? After all, ran the argument, who would you want alongside you in the trenches. Gary Lineker or Vinnie Jones? I put this to Dave Bassett.

'Football isn't in the trenches, though. Football has its violent moments, it has its artistic moments, its skilful moments, its bad moments. It's made up of a blend. You know, the generals don't sit in the trenches, do they? They correct things from a distance and they use their brains as well. If all of a sudden you're saying there's a big punch-up starting, yes, you want Arnold Schwarzenegger there with you, or a Fash who can handle himself. You don't want some wimp alongside you if you're about to be beaten up by thugs. On the other hand, you don't want a thicko when you're trying to work out your maths exam. Sometimes you need a strategist.

'So this "who would you rather have in the trenches?" debate is really a side question in football. You build a blend. You like your players to be competitive. Football is a competitive game – tennis, any sport is competitive. You want to win. And there's nothing wrong with winning and wanting to win. To some, competitiveness is a dirty word, but competition is always there. Life is a competition. You go for a job and there's only one person who's going to get it. If there's fifty of you, then forty-nine are going to be disappointed. There's a lot of crap talked about competition. You've got to be competitive. Life is competitive. There are losers and winners in every walk of life. There's an attractive bird and two blokes are after her. One's going to get her and one's not.'

Actually, some of the more co-operative, team-spirited players have found a way round that last dilemma, but as this is a football book and not a sex manual, I'll not elaborate on it here. As for not having Golden Gary alongside you . . .

'Gary Lineker's been a winner. He's loaded, isn't he? He's a millionaire. In his quiet way he's very competitive. He's played for England, he's scored all those goals. He wouldn't have been able to do it if he wasn't competitive. He don't give his money away, does he? He ain't a charity or anything like that! So he is competitive. People point to the fact that he's never been booked and that's a very good record to have, but it doesn't mean you're not competitive.'

Have players in this mould been a particular challenge to manage?

'Not really, no. Sides have always had "the man who can sort things out", get a few tackles in. That's part and parcel of the game. They're about now. You've got your Inces, your Dennis Wises. [Paul Ince, of course, popped off to Italy to teach them a thing or two.] All sides have got them and that's part of the game. Unfortunately the game is changing now. I think it's a game for pansies now. There's not the tackling about that was part of the game before, and I think it's losing its appeal to people because it's becoming a non-contact sport. That's why it'll never take off in America. Most Americans think football is for pansies, because there's no physical contact. They're used to their American football when they smash into one another; they love heavyweight boxing, the baseball . . . they'll have a few punch-ups, tell the referee he's a wanker and so on. The Americans I speak to say that with football, there's nothing in it for them. No physical contact, you're not allowed to have a go at the ref . . . to be honest, I don't see that football's got a cat in Hell's chance of taking off in the States.

'But you mustn't judge a person from what you see on the field. You can see a different fella on the field from off it. They can be two different characters. They cross that line and they become a different animal or a different person because of the involvement. A person could be a horrible bloke off the field, and on it be skilful and graceful, and similarly be a marvellous fella off it and a lunatic on the field. Players are under the microscope more than ever now because of football being our national sport. Some can live with it, but occasionally one will snap. There are punch-ups in pubs every night of the week if you go out in Sheffield, Leeds, London . . . people getting stabbed and everything else, yet when a footballer's involved, it's big news. Someone stabs a copper in the East End and you don't hear much about it because no one knows who it is. Dennis Wise has a fight with a taxi driver and it's front-page news.'

But back to on-pitch aggression. Duncan Ferguson, for example, although he had a record of criminal incidents off the pitch stacked up against him, was finally put away for something that happened on the pitch. No player seems above it all. Not since Gary Lineker retired, anyway. Even Gary's friend Gazza found himself at the mercy of trial by television in a match against Aberdeen. Although the referee had done nothing during the match, another official (the referee supervisor) complained, and film of the match was scrutinised for overenthusiastic elbow-barging and a possible head-butting incident à la Fergie. Although he got away with it that time, he was to pick up a phenomenal amount of bookings as the season went on. Many (Celtic supporters in particular, funnily enough) felt that a few red cards should have accompanied the yellow ones, but these at least were not forthcoming.

One of the problems may be that it's difficult to separate commitment from violence in such a physical and passionate game. Gazza, fighting his way back from injury, had a lot to prove to people who were saying he was past his prime and were writing him off. Could his drive to show they were wrong have spilled over into ungentlemanly conduct? I asked Leicester's Mark McGhee, a veteran of the Scottish game, who had not so long ago still been playing it himself, about the distinction between playing with a lot of heart and simply destroying anything and anyone who gets in your way. Can players sometimes confuse commitment with putting the boot in?

'I think that is a real problem. Managers, players, coaches and the public in general have in the past confused aggression and commitment to the point where they've become almost the same thing. I think what we really need on the football field is commitment. Now, with commitment come situations where you need to be aggressive, but aggression to me – and I have had to explain this to my players many, many times – can mean a number of things. You can be aggressive with the ball, without anyone else being involved. You can control the ball aggressively, you can pass the ball aggressively, you can tackle, head the ball, shoot aggressively. Every element of the game can and should be done aggressively. What that means to me, what it represents, is *concentration.* That's a word which goes better with aggression than commitment. But that's where the confusion lies. Commitment is going for the fifty-fifty ball, it's going and sticking your head in when other heads are going in there, running for ninety minutes, running back when you've been forward, getting forward when you've been back. That's commitment. Going out and playing well when you're under pressure, when the team's under pressure. That's commitment. But aggression is something else. Jumping up and punching somebody or pushing somebody isn't the kind of aggression we need on the football field – that's hooliganism. All clubs should have committed players. One of the reasons Leicester went down last year was that we don't have enough committed players who play with aggression.'

What about some of the players Mark played with at Celtic, players who could put themselves about a bit?

'Those players like Peter Grant – Grantie – Rambo [Alan McInally], Big Roy [Aitken] and the others. They had *commitment*. That's why they were never sent off. Mo Johnston was aggressive, but Mo Johnston was aggressive in that he controlled and shot the ball and passed aggressively. Gordon Strachan is aggressive, but he's not a *hooligan.* He's aggressive in that he runs after you aggressively, controls the ball aggressively and passes the ball aggressively. That to me is the sort of aggression that I need in my team.

> 'I see games up in Scotland and I think there is generally more commitment up there than there is, certainly, in many English players. I think, even in the lower leagues, although the playing isn't as good, the players aren't as good as most English players, they're more passionate and play with a bit more commitment.'

Perhaps the 'pansies' that the English game is throwing up should pop north of the border for a few lessons in taking it seriously. Certainly, since the annual England–Scotland fixture bit the dust, some of the passion seems to have vanished from the game.

But can we really separate passion from hooliganism, commitment from violent aggression? We can try, but how far we get may be limited, for some players more than others. Quite early in the season, the *Independent* carried an amusing little story about psychologists in South America, who had discovered that testosterone in male supporters climbs when they have watched their team win and drops when it has lost. Because testosterone is the hormone linked with sex drive, this naturally led to lots of references to impotent Manchester City supporters and randy Geordies, particularly by the time the *Sunday Sport* got hold of the story. But these findings should have been no surprise to psychologists. All kinds of things can affect testosterone levels and, if you're a passionate supporter, how your team is performing can certainly affect how you'll end up performing. Yet testosterone is also responsible for a lot of the behaviour concerned with competitive aggression and violence. Watching your team win is just as likely to lead to a punch-up as it is to all-night sex marathons.

Without practice, it's hard to manage the emotions associated with these surges in testosterone. Among the highest levels ever recorded in people were found in American ice hockey players, a game which is fiercely competitive and, not to put too fine a point on it, bloody violent. Even *defining* the sort of aggression that is required on the pitch can be hard, as Mark McGhee pointed out. Do players feel randy, heroic, focused on winning or in the mood for some aggro? Or some confused combination of these? A player like Gazza may be fighting to make his mark, to defend his sense of dignity and honour like William Wallace in *Braveheart* (the Paul Gascoigne-as-Mel Gibson photo opportunity was not neglected). Instead it comes out as violent conduct. It's hard not to feel some sympathy (unless you're an Aberdeen supporter).

And if we can understand unruly conduct in a player like Gazza, whose knee injury in 1991 which started all his problems was, of course, also the result of commitment overspilling into physical aggression, can we really be so hard on Vinnie and Julian?

Vinnie's present manager, Joe Kinnear had this to say:

> 'Providing you play it to the letter of the law, it's all right. Every single team that has ever been successful has had one or two of these so-called hard men. But these men also need to be able to play. I mean, Dave McKay [a former Spurs colleague from Joe's playing days] had a reputation; people said he was a "hard man" and he got stuck with that. But he was *more* than that. That's the sad thing about it. He was a very talented player, as I think Smithy was at Liverpool [Tommy Smith]. He could pass it, dribble it, come out of it, had vision, and I think all that stuff was pushed aside because he got a reputation for just being a hard man. Sometimes Dave Batty falls into the category in the modern game now. People get pigeon-holed and those that come to see them come to expect that type of performance all the time and if they don't see the aggression, they think a player's not doing it. Yet he's often contributing in other ways.
>
> 'People only ever analyse Vinnie in terms of how aggressive he is. When he got sent off when playing for Wales, journalists had a field day. People don't see that he's very effective in the modern game today. Vinnie is very effective at set-plays, which is a major part of football today. He's good in

the air, he's strong, he's a leader, he's a much better passer of the ball than people give him credit for. Paul Ince, he's another one with that kind of reputation, but he's a good player. You can see the work rate. He's a box-to-box man in the middle of the park, which is needed nowadays because the game is so quick. If you asked any manager who was honest what he wanted of his midfield players, he would say he'd like two Paul Inces in there and a Paul Gascoigne. You wouldn't have three Paul Gascoignes – unless you were Ossie Ardiles or someone like that!'

Ah yes, Ossie! A manager journalists loved to interview and clubs loved to sack. The man who invented the upside-down Christmas tree formation involving everybody up front tapering off to one defender or less. More about him, no doubt, as this tome unfolds. To return to the subject of hard men, they don't have it all hard, as Joe pointed out:

'But I'm happy with some of this, because a reputation buys such players more time. I think they're very fortunate people in some respects, because they have this intimidation about them. I try to tell our players: "Use it! If people don't want to come in and tackle you, then you're quite happy. You've always got the ball and you've always got control." The secret is to turn that to our advantage and keep doing what you're good at.

'So the only thing I regret is that these players don't get the credit they deserve. I mean, I admire these players. Any team that's going to be a Championship-winning side needs them. Vinnie is a character, and we have characters at this club by design, rather than accident. I bought him back from Chelsea to give us that something extra. I felt the responsibility for all that was mainly falling on John Fashanu's shoulders and he was moving more to television and promoting himself, with

Gladiators and everything else that he was doing. We had lost a lot of players and even though the spark was still there, we needed someone to ignite it a little more. When I took him from Chelsea, there were a few eyebrows raised, people saying "Oh no! They've gone back to what they were years ago", before I came here. Yet he's come here, ignited that spark. I love the guy, he's very popular with the players and he's even picked up one or two international caps late in his life.'

By the end of the season, it appeared that the leopards had been capable of changing their spots slightly, after all. As Jim Smith put it: 'To be fair, from what I gather, both Vinnie Jones and Julian Dicks have had less bookings this year than ever before, so obviously the penny's dropped. That's the value of keeping talking to players.'

I was going to leave it there, but the last word should probably go to Joe Kinnear's wife, Bonnie: 'Vinnie is a pussycat,' she said. 'You couldn't meet a nicer player.'

I'm sure I join Vinnie in hoping that such comments don't lose him his reputation.

5: Eurovision Gong Contest

'My, my! At Waterloo, Napoleon did surrender
Oh yes! And I have met my destiny in quite a similar way.'

Abba (although John Major seems to have
had a hand in those lyrics)

My, my indeed! Dear oh dear oh dear! When football historians look back at how British clubs performed in European competition, 1995 will not exactly stand out as a vintage year. There's nothing like the continentals rubbing our noses in it (and when I say *our*, I was born in Prague, so who am I to feel the same sense of national humiliation my friends feel?) to get the doom-and-gloom merchants out on the streets wailing, gnashing their teeth and generally proclaiming that the end of football is nigh.

Has it just been bad luck? Or is there more to it than that?

I have concentrated on Scottish clubs for this chapter, but this doesn't disguise in any way the fact that the English clubs were just as disappointing. In the UEFA Cup, English clubs were all scalped by early November, with the notable exception of Nottingham Forest, who weren't scalped until rather later – but well and truly scalped they were. Manchester United had, in fact, been knocked out even earlier, not even making it through the first round. Rotor Volgograd beat them on the away goals rule. Liverpool, the side everyone had been tipping to come out top of the Premier League before the season began, were beaten by Brondby, the first time an English club side had lost to a Danish one. Leeds, the side which, after striker Tony Yeboah's remarkable goals, had been added to many people's lists as possible Premiership winners shortly after the season started, lost 8–3 on aggregate to PSV Eindhoven, their worst ever aggregate defeat in European competition. In the Cup Winners' Cup, Everton managed to get rave reviews for holding Feynoord to a nil–nil draw at home, in a performance which, had it been the English national side responsible, would have had the papers baying for the manager's crucifixion, but then blew it by losing 1–0 on the away leg. Last season's Premier League champions, Blackburn Rovers, have simply never won a European match at all in modern times, their swan song from the Champions' League being a game against Spartak Moscow in which a fight erupted between two of the club's own players.

There was really very little joy to be had, especially as UEFA began to mutter about whether a country whose clubs turn out such feeble performances deserved to have so many of its clubs admitted into the competition. And in Scotland, things were no better.

Plucky little Raith Rovers fell to Bayern Munich. This wasn't as bad as all that. In fact, Danny Lennon even got a goal. Everyone had been expecting Raith not to make it through the first round. They were only in the competition in the first place because they had beaten Celtic in the previous season's Coca-Cola Cup. On penalties! Just how many miracles do you want?

No, the real disappointment was for Celtic and Rangers. Both clubs' fans had high hopes at the beginning of the season and both saw their dreams not so much dashed as put through a blender.

For both clubs, success in European cup competition had been the stuff of dreams, but for slightly different reasons. Celtic had been the first British club to win a European trophy when, under Jock Stein's management, they won the European Cup in 1967, beating Inter in the final. Those halcyon days also coincided with unprecedented success in domestic competition (an as-yet-unbeaten nine league championships in a row). Since then, success had begun to leak away, and in recent years had been gushing out so quickly that Red Adair couldn't have stopped it. A board reviled by the fans and satirised to great effect in the club's fanzine, *Not the View*, had, in the opinions of many, misinterpreted Brother Walfrid's original intentions in setting up the club. The idea had been to be charitable towards poor families in the East End of Glasgow. Those on the club's board had apparently assumed that they had been the families in question and had helped themselves for years as the club's fortunes on the field took a nose dive. Having dismissed the popular Billy McNeill as manager, the board appointed Liam Brady. Brady had been one of Ireland's most popular players. He had never managed in his life.

'The crazy thing about football that makes it different from any other walk of life is the fact that if you have been a successful player, clubs automatically think you're going to be a successful football manager,' says the present holder of that title, Tommy Burns. 'With no experience of management, you suddenly become a manager in the football world because it is perceived that if someone played for a club and was a good footballer, you should give him a job as a manager. There's no getting away from it. It's very difficult to suddenly step into something like that and to find yourself in charge of a lot of things that you don't really know a great deal about.'

Brady's reign was not a success. Sacked by the club, he went on to manage Brighton where, early into this season, he was also dismissed following a disastrous run of results and being held to a draw by Canvey Island. Then came Lou Macari. That didn't work either, and his defensive, long-ball tactics seemed totally at odds with Celtic's reputation for fast, attacking, defence-free play.

Tommy Burns joined from Kilmarnock, where he had become a manager. Looking back on his career, he sees it as a process of evolution:

'Being involved with a football club since you were fourteen, fifteen years old and playing for them for seventeen, eighteen years, then playing four or five years somewhere else, it's basically all you know. It's just a gradual progression. A lot of the time you'll go from being a player into coaching and eventually to assistant manager or manager. For me it just seemed a progression, but things came up for me early. I became a player-manager early in life. Then I got the chance to manage Celtic. It's a question of opportunities arising and it's a learning process.'

Tommy Burns clearly loved playing for Celtic. The club and its traditions were always close to his heart. Was it always at the back of his mind that one day he'd want to come back and manage the Bhoys in green and white?

'No, not at all! Kilmarnock had a different manager when I first went there, and I was quite happy just playing for them. Then, all of a sudden, they sacked him and asked me to take over and so basically I just did it out of friendship with the chairman. No one else would do it because there were only six games to go of the season. Those six games went very well for me and they offered me the job, so that was it.'

But back to Celtic's decline. At the time they acquired (some would say poached) Tommy from Kilmarnock, fans' morale was at rock bottom. Never mind having thrown away the hope of qualifying to play in Europe on a regular basis, for many fans, a victory in the Tennents Sixes was the new height of attainable ambition. They had lost their Parkhead stadium and were reduced to borrowing Hampden Park every other Saturday (not as ridiculous as it sounds, given the Scottish national team have to borrow it, too – it belongs to club side Queen's Park). Burns was the man to spearhead a renaissance. Having won the Scottish Cup and only narrowly missed out on the Coca-Cola Cup (that penalty shoot-out with Raith I mentioned earlier) in his first season as Celtic manager, the fans looked to him as someone to lead them out of the darkness and on to new-found glory. They had been so far down it couldn't have got worse if the board had appointed Homer Simpson as manager, but with Burns, a hero from his playing days and a manager who had proved his worth at a smaller club, they were given real hope that the glory days under Stein were not the club's last. There was also a new stadium and a new chairman, the instantly caricaturable Fergus McCann.

Tommy Burns, like his former Celtic team-mate, Leicester manager Mark McGhee, is never one to throw caution to the wind: 'Well, we feel that circumstances have taken over and basically a new board has come in. There's a new stadium built, there are all the debts inherited from the last regime and with all these things happening, people just expect everything is suddenly going to change overnight. There have been a lot of different things to contend with – building this new stadium has cost an astronomical amount of money. We're moving slowly but surely forward, but we've still got a long, long way to go and a lot of hard work ahead of us.'

While all this had been going on, Rangers had been going from strength to strength on the other side of Glasgow. They were now within two championships of Celtic's nine-in-a-row record. But in European competition things had been different. What did Burns make of the prevailing view that Celtic's early performances in the Cup Winners' Cup were much more encouraging than Rangers' in the Champions' League qualifier?

> 'Well, it has to be said that they're in a much more difficult arena, if you like – dealing with the real top quality. We're there because we won the Scottish Cup. Anybody can win a cup. If you get a decent run, you can snatch it. We were fortunate enough to win it for the first time in five or six years,

which gave us a great lift at the club, but at the same time we know that anything we get in Europe will be a bonus. Getting through the first round was a bonus, and now we play against Paris St Germain so if we get anything out of that, it'll be a bonus as well. But *here* is the main priority. It's nice to be there [in Europe], but I think we're still a fair bit away from being able to really be a force.'

Rangers, of course, are already a force, in the Scottish game at least. Not for them Celtic's desire to get on top of the domestic game and make that their own – Rangers have already done that! No, European success is the big one. It's proof that the club is more than just a big fish in a small pond. Not only that, but in recent years, it has been proving very elusive.

Rangers had their first taste of European glory in 1972, winning the Cup Winners' Cup. In 1993, they reached the equivalent of the semi-finals of the European Cup. Then things began to go wrong. The club began to fall at the first hurdle, something which manager Walter Smith remembers as particularly painful.

'The players look forward to the challenge of quality opposition. There's absolutely no doubt about that. Last season, we got knocked out by AEK Athens. That was as damaging a result as we have ever had. Psychologically, that was difficult to handle. People now expect us to win things in Scotland, but we have to put that properly into the broader context of Europe. Two seasons ago, we did well in the European Cup, we got near the final. We went ten games without defeat, which is a terrific run in that competition, and it did show that if we can get a team together, we can compete at that level. The following season, we were knocked out in the preliminary round – you have to take the whole of Scottish football into context, because the other clubs did badly as well – but we were a mockery. So you've got one year when we could have got to the European Cup final with a little bit of luck, the next we were out in the preliminary round and people were saying Scottish football is rubbish, it's garbage. But you've got to adopt a middle line. I never allow people to get too carried away when they win and, by the same token, I don't like them to get too depressed when they lose. I've tried to take that middle line, take a sensible approach, all the time that I've been manager here. I think that makes it easier to handle situations like when you're knocked out of a cup.

'It's interesting that everybody always asks "What do you do after a defeat?", but what do you do after you *win*? Nobody asks that. How does a club handle winning? That can be as big a problem to the club manager as losing. In losing, you're inclined to show anger. You're inclined to sound off in a manner which players would appreciate. Players expect that, and you can do all that. But how do you handle winning? Mishandling that can have as adverse an effect as mishandling losing. You've always got to show that you're pleased when the team has won and upset when it has lost, but you do need some middle line. You can't get too carried away when winning or too upset when losing. If you can keep that balance, you can handle the situations that crop up.'

None of this is helped by the press, of course, for whom a team's performance has either been the Eighth Wonder of the World or a disaster of Titanic proportions. Smith is well aware of this: 'That is part of management that you have to keep pointing out to people. People's perceptions of games are sometimes nowhere near the manager's perception, and that's a part of the job that you have to keep an eye on, talk to your staff about and make sure they don't pay too much attention to what they read.'

So, don't take the criticism too hard, but don't get caught up in believing all of your own publicity either. Scotland fans who still have memories of the 1978 World Cup campaign will vouch for that. As the only British side that had qualified for the final stages, Scotland's Tartan Army got so carried away that they really thought they had a good chance of winning the trophy. If that expectation was unrealistic, so too was the morbid gloom and vitriolic press dissection of the team which followed. Walter Smith is no Ally MacLeod. He makes sure the downs are not too low, by keeping the ups from getting too high.

> 'So we went from reaching a high one season to a low the next. It didn't affect us so badly that season, because we were still on a bit of a high from doing so well the previous season. For the past couple of seasons, we've been changing players round; we've had a bad run of injuries but a bit of domestic success over that period. Now we're looking forward to getting back into playing European games. But what I always keep saying to people, and they don't always take it on board, is to take a sensible view. People sometimes find that boring. They say: "Let's take a critical path or let's take the praise path. One or the other. Don't sit in the middle." But the margin of error in European matches – all international matches – at the moment is very slight indeed. There's absolutely no doubt about that, not even any argument about it. You can have a very good team and go into the European Cup and have two or three draws and we could win a game and lose a game and not qualify for the quarter-finals. That would be a middle-of-the-road performance. That, in many people's eyes, would be OK. But the conception of Rangers Football Club, the way that everybody talks about them, is that they can *win the European Cup!* We had a pre-season tournament here with matches against Steaua Bucharest and Sampdoria, and we won both matches. For the following couple of days, it was "Rangers Set For Europe!", "Rangers are among the favourites to win the European Cup!" Now, the year before, we were duffers. We were nowhere. Now, it's good to be back

in the European Cup, but we're still some way off being potential winners. You've got to give us a chance. We've been drawn against a section that will *show* us how good we are at the present moment. I think we can do well. We should, given that we've got all the players out on the pitch and we look forward to it, but sometimes unrealistic expectation is carried into these European games, and it puts extra pressure on the club, which I don't think is always a fair one.'

Indeed, when expectation is so high, playing against a little side which no one seriously regards as a threat can almost be more of a pressure than playing against one of the acknowledged giants of Europe.

'Well, that happened to us, after losing two years on the trot to little sides in the European Cup. This season we were drawn against Famagusta and people just thought "Ach! Easy team! You'll beat them without any problem," but I've never experienced the kind of tension that surrounds the actual preliminary game in the competition. It's probably one of the most tense games we ever had to prepare for. The financial loss to a bigger club is enormous if you get caught out, so you have that to worry about on the one hand and there's the footballing side as well. That tension gets to the players on the field. That's one match where I've seen it happen. When you *need* to qualify . . . I've seen it in English teams, too. Leeds United, Manchester United and Arsenal have all failed to qualify in the preliminary round. That is the point I make to people. We've failed as well, and we've had more opportunities than these teams, so I don't like to make direct comparisons, but what people do fail to realise is the level of tension in these preliminary rounds. I mean, Manchester United are a better team than Galatasaray [currently the stomping ground of Walter Smith's predecessor as Rangers manager, Graeme

Souness] and they lost, albeit on an away goal. But they *lost*. All I kept reading in the English papers was "Twelve Million Quid. They're going to make twelve million" . . . and then all of a sudden, three days later, they've lost twelve million. Now, that kind of amount probably isn't true, but it does get to people. You can be out of the European Cup before your league campaign has really started. A lot of stress.'

'Yes, it must have been a big blow to them,' says Tommy Burns of Rangers' inability to qualify for the Champions League stage the previous two seasons. 'It's been a heavy price to pay. But that's something I'd be only too glad to become involved in, the preliminary round of the European Cup!'

Well, grabbing Rangers' Championship crown would have to come first, before any of that was possible. In the meantime, there was Paris St Germain in the UEFA Cup. At least Paris isn't too exotic. Mark McGhee recalls his days as a player in European competition: 'They get away with more gamesmanship at an international level, because of the distances travelled and differences in culture, than you get in the domestic game. Then there is the food. When I was with Celtic, we played against Dynamo Kiev, just after the nuclear power plant accident at nearby Chernobyl. I scored that night and was man of the match. Got a lovely big silver salver. We brought our own food, rather than try the local chicken! We took stuff from the Grosvenor Hotel in Glasgow and the guy from there came and prepared it for us. I'd done that before. I went with Aberdeen to Albania and they did the same.'

It's always a mistake to rely on food being available in any appreciable amounts in what used to be the Eastern Bloc: 'Well, we didn't do it when I played in Prague!' said McGhee.

Just as well! I was raised on Prague's food myself. And the beer is dead cheap.

Anyway, I digress. Back to Rangers . . .

After the pressure of having to put on a good show in the

preliminary round, where the stress certainly showed against Famagusta, a Cypriot side vastly inferior on paper, Rangers found themselves facing a particularly difficult combination of teams in the Champions' League. They were alongside Steaua Bucharest, whom they had entertained and beaten in the pre-season tournament at Ibrox, Borussia Dortmund, and the mighty Juventus, a club familiar to Gazza from his days at Lazio.

Looking back, Walter Smith's sense of moderation definitely helps. Rangers were knocked out largely as a result of two hugely disappointing performances against Juventus. A 4–0 home defeat was the worst in 35 years of European competition. Away, they had managed a single goal, while Juventus got another four. Rangers were comprehensively outplayed. Paul Gascoigne didn't get a look-in in a game he described as a 'tanking'. He was later to score a spectacular goal against Steaua Bucharest, but it was not enough to save the club's skin. The Juventus manager didn't mince words: 'It was as easy as I expected,' he commented.

Celtic, in the end, did no better. Lacking the pressure that comes of having made early exits from Europe in previous years (when they hadn't been in the competition in the first place), some fancied them to turn on a better performance than Rangers. They held Paris St Germain to a one goal lead in France and the green half of Glasgow was confident that they'd outshine the blue. A 3–0 home defeat put paid to all that.

The 4–0 defeat of Rangers at home to Juventus and the 3–0 defeat of Celtic at home to Paris St Germain came within a day of one another, in a week when supporters across Glasgow had ample excuse to pile on the gloom. As far as making an impact in Europe was concerned, it was 'That's all, folks!' for another year. Of course, Manchester United and Blackburn had done even worse, but that wasn't much to sugar the pill.

Tommy Burns and particularly Walter Smith faced outraged fans and scathing journalists. Yet, being realistic, the former had seen Europe as 'a bonus', an agreeable luxury, but not one to deter the team from the task at hand – the pursuit of domestic honours. The latter had been wary of excessive expectation. Did anything good come of it all?

'Maybe they'll realise they're not as good as they thought they were,' suggested Smith to one journalist. It was the voice of pained realism in a country whose football supporters are famed for their dedication and their passion. When Rangers and, if we are to be generous, Celtic, have dominated the domestic scene for so long, it's hard to accept just how small the pond that holds these big fish can be. But Walter Smith knew it and he accepted it. Not for him the excesses of media hype. He knows that reaching the equivalent of the semi-finals in 1993 was just as unusual as getting knocked out in the preliminaries. Not the norm, by any means. Something of a lucky break.

Away from the hysteria, he still found time for optimism. 'I received some good news today,' he pointed out. 'The kettle's working.'

6: It's Very Dashing, The Continental

'In Italy you couldn't eat bananas and ice cream. In England they don't care what you eat – only what you say.'

Anders Limpar

'You know what the funniest thing about Europe is? It's the little differences . . .'

John Travolta's Oscar-nominated observations in *Pulp Fiction* related mainly to the bill of fare at continental McDonald's outlets, but could easily have been applied to the fact that football management across the Channel seems subtly distinct from what is practised on these shores. With the demolition of Nottingham Forest by Bayern Munich, home fans having seen the side go down 5–1 at the City Ground, making the score 7–2 to the German side on aggregate, the Great White Hope of British club football was finally flat out on the canvas, completely unconscious. There were few merry men around Sherwood Forest that night, and anyone who had hoped for the return of European success on the scale witnessed under Cloughie in the seventies was to have their hopes cut short. The cynics said that the boys from the City Ground had been lucky to get as far as they did. The club had played quite commendably in the first leg, away, and had certainly done considerably better than the other British clubs involved in European competitions, but inexperience and the do-or-die enthusiasm which can accompany it had, critics maintained, worked in the club's favour, until the trick was rumbled and the steam ran out. Unfavourable comparisons with European clubs abounded and the usual moaning and groaning about the state of British football was an inevitability.

Nevertheless, the number of continental players coming across to play in the English and Scottish leagues had never been higher, suggesting that there must be something going for the game on these isles. Indeed, a story went around that this very fact had somewhat scuppered Forest captain Stuart Pearce's attempt to motivate his players in the battle against the Germans: 'Above all,' it's claimed he said, 'remember you're British!' He then looked around the dressing room and it dawned on him that this might not have been the right thing to say considering so many players were nothing of the sort.

Could we learn from the continentals, though? Many managers agree that we can. One who is in no doubt is Celtic's Tommy Burns.

Burns is one manager who is not afraid to admit that the learning process doesn't stop when you sign the dotted line. He took time out from his holiday before the season began to visit the Netherlands and find out more about the coaching methods employed at Ajax, a club with considerable European success, placing particular emphasis on their youth coaching policy. For a club like Celtic, known traditionally for growing its own talent, only recently joining the bigger players in the transfer market, and still very cautious about overspending (a few years previously, prior to a bit of a spree by Liam Brady, it could have been argued that the club was cautious about spending any money at all!), such curiosity has invaluable potential in the longer run.

'When you look at some of our younger players, we've had some fantastic results,' Burns told me. 'We beat the Rangers youth team – the Under Eighteens – five–nil at Celtic Park and the quality of our young players was there for all to see.'

It was no surprise, then, that, in the middle of the season, Burns was off again, this time to Turin, where he found out more about the coaching methods employed at Juventus.

'It was an education,' he said of his travels. 'Ajax proved to be more technical, while Juventus were physically strong and organised, but both were tactically advanced.'

Such a move is an unusual one by British club standards. Traditionally, the general feeling has been that the game was invented over here, so we can't possibly have anything to learn from other countries' clubs. However, this view seems to be changing. Celtic have as strong a heritage as any club – they were, after all, the first British club to bring back the European Cup – but their manager felt he, and his players, had something to learn. After the performances of British clubs in Europe this year, it is likely that several other managers will be making such trips if they are not already doing so, probably greater in number than managers from the rest of Europe heading on fact-finding trips over here. At least there are the European Championships being held here to lure continental managers across the Channel!

'What Ajax can achieve with their youth policy, we would like to do at Celtic. We have some excellent sixteen-year-old players, so we're on the way,' Tommy Burns promised. But it isn't just the emphasis on developing young talent that he feels is a particular strength of some of the clubs he has visited. The whole approach to management seems to be different abroad.

> 'The reason it's a different kind of approach is that the manager in this country takes on the role of manager, coach and whatever else, whereas, on the continent, the manager is generally the one who looks after the financial side of things at a football club and it's the coach that basically runs the football team. In Scotland, England and Ireland, the manager does both. But I think it's only a matter of time before this country falls in with the continentals in the fact that a club will bring in somebody to coach the team and

> then another guy will be instructed to deal with the finance and so on and so on.'

Of course, the England manager's title has been changed to Chief Coach to reflect this change. Will Scotland follow suit?

'I think so,' Burns said. 'Definitely – at the bigger clubs, anyway. Maybe not so much at the smaller clubs.'

Even at a smaller club like Crystal Palace, this kind of demarcation seems to be doing the trick. Dave Basset's results on taking over (see chapter ten) speak for themselves, but it was clear that there were others at the club also connected with different aspects of management and coaching, former manager Steve Coppell among them. Shortly after he took over, I was able to ask 'Harry' Basset about whether Tommy Burns' views on the changing roles of managers are being taken up:

> 'Yes, I think to some extent it's already happening. Some managers nowadays are not coaches and they do the transfer activity, the contracts and all of the admin while others do more of the coaching, so it's a slightly similar thing to what they've got on the continent, except that here the manager is perhaps a bit more of a figurehead. In Europe, the coach is the figurehead for the team, in charge of the tactics, which are seen as very important, and usually more well known than the manager. The manager tends to be slightly less known if he's dealing with the business end of things. It's the opposite over here – except that many managers take on a lot of the coaching and the tactics *as well* as the financial aspects. It all depends on what a chairman wants from his manager, really.'

A classic case in this country is, of course, Birmingham City, where the roles of business manager Karen Brady and team manager Barry Fry are very distinct and where the media and press seem much more interested in Brady as a figurehead, possibly because large double-page spreads of Barry Fry are not considered quite as easy on the eye. (Though tastes may differ on this. The *Sunday Sport* tends to give equal coverage to both and this surely can't be just because Birmingham's chairman happens to own it.)

And who was set to do what at Palace, following Harry's arrival?

> 'Well, I'm the manager and I shall make those decisions as necessary because that's my responsibility as manager. Ultimately, the buck stops with me. The other members of staff work in their areas and if I feel at any time that we should change things round a bit or modify anything, then we'll act accordingly. I'm not going to make any hasty decisions. I've got to look at things between now and the end of the season and if I feel that roles need to change to build on people's strengths, then I'll make those decisions.'

The 'buck-stops-here' definition of management probably highlights the different approaches in Britain and on the continent. Here, when everything falls to bits, the manager gets the sack. Over there, if the same happens, the coach tends to go and the manager stays put. On television's *Sport in Question*, former Arsenal manager George Graham pointed out that the situation which led to his dismissal from the club, the receipt of a 'gift' from a continental agent, would not have happened to a European coach-style manager, as these people's responsibility is only to name players they would like to buy, rather than to suggest or even set a price as is the case in this country. Arguably, in the UK the manager is given more responsibility, but he is therefore more exposed to potential financial jiggery-pokery.

Not everyone, however, would be as strongly in favour of devolving the business management and coaching aspects of football management in this country quite as starkly. Tommy Burns' former Celtic team-mate, Mark McGhee, had this to say:

'I think the European approach of splitting these roles is something that would suit some clubs and suit certain people. It's not something that suits me, particularly. I feel that, as a manager, I'm somewhere between the two. I feel that, in order to understand what's happening here at Wolves, I have to have control – or certainly an influence – on what's happening with the financial and business side of the club, especially those parts relating directly to the football. I certainly don't demand total responsibility for the coaching. I have a guy here, Colin Lee, who I regard as a world-class coach, and I give Colin a very, very free hand. Colin has a different schedule from me, he works different hours. At, say, half past two in the afternoon, he's gone. He'll have finished training, had lunch with the players and he'll be gone. But I know he's sitting at home at that time, not only thinking about what's going to be happening in the next couple of weeks, but also about tomorrow. I know he'll come to me with a couple of things and say: "Did you think of this?" or "Did you think of that?" Later on tonight, I'll be doing the same thing, and we'll compare notes.

'But, in terms of day-to-day training, Colin has a bit more time to sit with his book and his manuals and to come up with ideas on how to coach and how to organise sessions that are going to help with the concerns that I have. So, in a sense, if I feel a certain aspect of the team needs attention, he's the one who gets the tools out. I'm the one who diagnoses what's going on and he's the one who's given licence – probably more licence than may be the case at some other clubs – to make repairs.'

What about the increasing trend for players to go more-or-less straight into management, without spending a long period of time coaching, as has been the traditional pattern in this country?

'Coaching and managing are two different things. They're

both, in a sense, vocational. You really have to want to be a coach – and to have the ability. I think managing is the same. There are some very good coaches who don't have the ability to manage a football club, and I think there are some managers who don't have the ability to coach all that well. That doesn't mean that they can't be managers. Different people bring different things to the table, as it were, and the important thing is that, when you put the pieces together, you have a complete picture. I believe that, with the people here at Wolves – Colin Lee, Mike Hookman, and the people I've "inherited" since I came here – plus my own input, I think we have that, and that's the important thing.

'As for the fact that people are moving into management younger these days, I think it's like any business in that sense – the people who run the business like and appreciate young, aggressive, ambitious managers. That seems to be true of any business, any company these days. Those who have the energy to want to go out and do the work are the best people to have.'

Are there other factors to recommend the continental approach to management? Wycombe Wanderers' Alan Smith certainly thinks so:

'The problem with being a football manager in this country – and I've said this a lot of times – is that there is no qualification associated with doing the job. In Europe, you have to be qualified and that'll take you three to seven years. That's true of most of the European countries including the Scandinavian countries. Over here, it's a job which anybody thinks they can do. If you're a doctor or an aircraft pilot or a chartered accountant, people know that not everybody can do it. With football management, you can ask practically everyone in the country, and they all think they can do the job. Now, if a qualification existed for doing it, such as a three- to seven-year course that you had to go on to become the manager of a Premier League team, it would make people think that it's not quite so easy just to go and do it.

'The big problem on the management side is that, while there are people who are very successful at it, there are too many who come into it who are in every sense simply not qualified to do it. Their sole qualification may just be that they have played two hundred league games, which unfortunately is not enough.

'If you look at Ron Noades, my chairman when I was at Crystal Palace, he would bring in all kinds of friends and acquaintances to do coaching jobs. While I was there, a guy was brought in to run our youth team system, seemingly because Noades knew him and he'd packed up work at British Telecom and could come in and do it. Now, with due respect, someone who's been working for British Telecom shouldn't come along and start running the youth team at Crystal Palace because Ron knows him. If there had been a set qualification which needed to be provided to enable someone to do that at a club, the situation would never have arisen.

'It would also make it harder for clubs to sack managers just like that. Look at Bradford sacking Lennie Lawrence. Has he really done that badly? Bradford were eighth in Division Two. Well, where *should* Bradford be? It seems to me, as an outsider, that eighth in Division Two is OK for Bradford. When Brian Horton was sacked by Manchester City, he hadn't done a bad job, though you could argue that he shouldn't have been appointed in the first place because Peter Reid, who came before him, hadn't done a bad job. Southampton are very interesting. Chris Nicholl was the manager there, and then they had Ian Branfoot and now Dave Merrington, and they're still no better off. It's been change for change's sake.

'The supporters do like a change. They're not particularly bothered who the manager really is. As long as he's successful, they're quite happy. It's almost like the Romans watching Christians being thrown to the lions. They don't really care who it is, just bring on the next one! You don't get people running round the streets of Bradford shouting "Good old Lennie Lawrence!" Having said that, Mike Walker got something like two hundred and fifty thousand pounds' compensation for leaving Everton, which isn't bad for a guy of forty who's been there for six months. You've got to look at that side to managerial hirings and firings in this country, too.

'I just think that, in the UK, to an outsider looking in, there is no logic at all to appointing football managers. Why Terry Westley was appointed manager at Luton, I just don't know. I don't think he had the qualification to do the job. I'm not saying I wanted it, because I didn't, but I genuinely don't see how promoting the guy who was the youth development officer to that position is going to help the club. That would never happen in Europe.

'People will pull out examples of players who have become successful managers. They'll say look at Keegan or Bryan Robson [though, as the season went on, and Middlesbrough's performances faltered, Robson's name figured less and less in such lists. Glenn Hoddle remained up there], but for as many people as have made a success of it, there are just as many who haven't: the Bobby Moores; the Geoff Hursts; the Bobby Charltons.'

Interestingly, while Bobby Charlton's attempts at management were never anything to write home about, his brother Jack seems to have done rather better during his stint as Ireland manager, which came to a close as this book was being written. Purists might have quibbled over his direct style, but as far as the supporters were concerned, canonisation was surely not too far away. Alan Smith concluded:

> 'Bobby Charlton was a great player, but when it came to management, he just couldn't do the job. It's quite a complex job – if you do it properly. Getting people to complete a period of training before they were qualified to do it would improve the quality of managers enormously in this country.'

Evidently, then, this is no time for Euroscepticism. When it comes to developing youth talent and introducing some kind of qualification to establish whether someone can do the job properly, the continentals are way ahead of us.

They may insist on dipping their French fries in mayonnaise, but when it comes to winning major European club competitions we'd better see what we can learn from them.

7: Who's In Charge, Here?

'To these nobody-somebodies, managers are, as they are frequently reminded, just employees. Big Ron is not in Who's Who, *nor are Cloughie or El Tel, although the publication is stuffed with directors, chairmen and vice-presidents of football clubs.'*

Mark Lawson, *Independent*

It's natural to think of the manager's job as one involving lots of interaction with players, and, depending on how many additional coaching staff exist at a club, with their various assistants. However, you only have to listen to any of the former managers who now make a living on the after-dinner speaking circuit and it becomes very apparent that there is an even more important relationship in the manager's life. How a manager gets on with the club's chairman (and they are *all* men, though the occasional female club director has begun to appear) is absolutely fundamental. The strength or the fragility of that relationship reverberates throughout the club, and will be felt at every level.

The chairman's vote of confidence has now become so synonymous with the kiss of death that the idea was used to advertise insurance. This suggests that in a great many cases, the relationship between chairman and manager is not a simple one, while in quite a few it is dysfunctional enough to warrant specialist counselling.

Effective communication, an understanding of how the other works and some level of trust, however that is qualified, become essential if this relationship, the bedrock on which any club thirsty for success can begin to build, is to be a healthy one. If a club is to win trophies, it has to be very healthy indeed. The odd hiccup or sniffle, and that health can deteriorate as rapidly as if it were under attack by a virulent plague.

Such a relationship, however much it may be hidden from public scrutiny, tends to be fairly well understood by those connected with a club. It soon becomes clear who is making the big decisions and who is just tagging along, whether one party can persuade the other or simply do their bidding, whether what exists is two-way dialogue or a gaffer who's 'just following orders'. If both individuals are strong-willed, forceful personalities, then the fans can just hope that they'll both be singing the same tune, or something is going to have to give.

Derby County's Jim Smith has worked with some of the most notorious chairmen in the game, including arguably the most notorious, the late but not universally lamented Robert Maxwell. It was at Maxwell's Oxford United that Jim Smith was able to win the League Cup, beating Queen's Park Rangers, a side he would go on to manage next. Ironically, Maxwell moved on to become chairman of Derby County afterwards, leaving Oxford United to other members of his family. Their paths were not to cross a second time, however. By the time 'The Bald Eagle' took up the managerial reins at Derby, all traces of the Maxwell dynasty had been washed away, if that's not a tasteless turn of phrase.

'At the end of the day, if you haven't got the support of your chairman, it's not going to last very long,' he maintains. 'Invariably, or at least in ninety per cent of the clubs you go to, it's the chairman-cum-owner-cum-everything that you're dealing with and if it's not a democratic board and you can't get on with your chairman, there's no point in working there, in all honesty.'

It is surely no coincidence that, of those managers interviewed for this book, the one at the most obviously successful football club also seemed to enjoy a relationship with his chairman that seemed little short of idyllic. Walter Smith confided:

> 'The relationship with your chairman is probably the most important one. It can make or break a manager. If both are pulling in the same direction then everybody else at the club looks at the chairman, looks at the manager and says: "Right! *That's* the way we're going." Players like to see clear direction. He leaves me to run the football side of things, I talk to him about everything involving the club. I have discussions with him every day.'

I mentioned Dave Bassett's problems early on in the season at Sheffield United.

> 'If there is any acrimony between the chairman and the manager – Alan Sugar and Terry Venables at Spurs, for example – or if you have a board that won't back you, you're looking at a football club in a state of panic. You've got no chance. None whatsoever.'

David Murray, the Rangers chairman, is widely recognised as the man who transformed the club from a struggling side to the club which has now been top of the league in Scotland seven times in a row. An entrepreneur who made his money, like Blackburn's Jack Walker, in scrap metal, it was his investment that led to the shining new stadium, sold out for every match, a team of star players and, if you're a Rangers supporter, a future that, as an unconnected advert for cellular phones once put it, looks bright – the future looks orange.

> 'That's the way Rangers have been run. I'm here. He's there. To all intents and purposes, we've always been together. The

people who run football clubs have personalities and have put in a lot of money. People say, "It's the chairman that buys the player." Well, it is. I'm happy with that. Now he doesn't buy a player alone. I recommend a player and then he goes and does the physical buying. I'm very happy for him to do that, because the amount of money concerned – both in terms of contracts and in terms of transfer fees – is huge. A football manager shouldn't be put in a position where he's okaying the expenditure of four and a half million quid.'

Would Mr Murray ever query the manager's recommendation?

'Oh yes! He'll say, "*Are you sure?*" and I'll say, "That's the player I want to go for." I'll give him my reasons. But there hasn't been too much of that recently.'

How many managers must drift off to sleep at night dreaming of that kind of relationship? For every David Murray, there are dozens of Sugars, Maxwells, Swaleses, Bateses . . .

Rangers' biggest rivals had come a long way towards regaining some of the respect they had lost over recent years, thanks to new chairman, Fergus McCann, who had replaced a board so derided that the consensus among fans was that they were keeping their money (of which there appeared to be not inconsiderable amounts) shut up in a biscuit tin. The old regime had been arguably the most hated of any British club, with a business brain worthy less of a board and more of two short planks. Compared to them, a mug punter dragged from a local bookies would probably have seemed a better bet to run the club.

McCann's reign thus far appears successful, but he is no Jack Walker, running the club at a loss and pouring in a personal fortune to buy players. What Blackburn achieved virtually overnight is unlikely to be a common experience. It needs someone with ridiculous amounts of money and a love of a club that transcends this wealth. Rather, McCann has come across as shrewd – a friend of mine once spotted him in a Glasgow hotel quibbling over the price of his breakfast on the bill, claiming he had not had cornflakes. On taking on the role, he specified that he would only do it for five years and then move on, leaving the club in a healthier state. This was in March 1994, so at the time of writing, he had served nearly half his stint. In this time, he presided over the biggest share issue ever seen in British football, and substantial rebuilding of Celtic's stadium, while the team were forced, much to his annoyance, to play all their home matches at Scotland's national stadium, Hampden Park. Fans can have few complaints except, perhaps, that so great is the new weight of expectation now, everyone wants success more immediately than may be realistic. McCann shares his surname with Arthur Daley's minder, and the club has certainly seemed safe in his hands.

Nevertheless, his relationship with manager Tommy Burns did not seem as trouble-free as that of David Murray with Walter Smith . . .

'I think it's fair to say that the chairman and I had our differences earlier on. However, we've now both settled down into what I believe is a better appreciation of the job that lies ahead for the club as a whole and also of each other's position,' was Tommy Burns' comment on the matter.

The papers like little better than stories of a feud between the boardroom and the bootroom. At Chelsea, chairman Ken Bates' disagreements with director Matthew Harding were extensively reported, along with the negative impact they inevitably had on Glenn Hoddle. Could this have been one of the major reasons that he was to walk away from club football and accept the England job? That it wasn't at least a consideration seems unlikely.

However, Tommy Burns will be comforted to observe that differences between manager and chairman can be ironed out so smoothly that it's hard to see how they could ever have started. In

Kevin Keegan's early days managing Newcastle, such was his frustration at not being given money to buy players (money he said he had been promised by chairman Sir John Hall) that he actually resigned and left the club – or was about to, when an emergency meeting enabled both parties to air their grievances and to come to a mutual understanding that, by all accounts, seems to have blossomed into one of the most firm manager–chairman relationships in the country. A lot more managers would, I'm sure, be keen to pull off a stunt like this but, unfortunately, not many of them have Keegan's money. They *need* their jobs.

How many bosses put up with chairmen who give them little support, moral or financial, to venture into the transfer market, and just have to grin and bear it because their job depends on it and they lack the financial security of some of the newer, richer ex-player managers, who always have that 'Hang on, I don't *need* to be doing this to make a living' ace up their sleeves?

Too many, I fear. Sometimes, however, relations become too strained to carry on the pretence any longer.

Yet another Smith, Alan, was adamant that harmony with the chairman is worth its weight in gold – something which was not exactly forthcoming during his time at Crystal Palace, where he frequently failed to see eye to eye with outspoken and controversial chairman Ron Noades.

> 'It probably is the most vital relationship within the club, without any doubt. But I never had a relationship with Ron. I didn't when I was the youth team manager, which made my life very, very difficult, and when I was reserve team manager, he made it equally difficult. It was in niggly sorts of ways. I think, in his heart of hearts he accepts that I was pretty good at what I did, but I believe he was a jealous type of man, nowhere near as self-confident as he comes across. I think he liked the thought of him and Coppell being together, he liked the names being linked. It was when it became a bit more the

Coppell–Smith thing that he didn't quite like that so much. But I think it is a very important relationship within a club, and if there is no relationship between manager and chairman, it will not work. There is only one winner, as we saw with Venables and Sugar and as you saw with Noades and Smith. It was inevitable. I knew it, but it was inevitable anyway. I had nothing to lose, quite frankly, which also bugged him, I think. I mean, the day I walked out of Palace was not a financial disaster for me and that probably bugged him.'

But who's *really* running the game? If the managers have to answer to their chairmen, to whom are the chairmen accountable?

The official answer is, of course, the Football Association, or its Scottish equivalent, the SFA. This in turn answers to the European governing body, UEFA, and ultimately to FIFA, the world authority. That, at any rate is the theory. How does it work in practice? Dave Bassett was never one to pull punches:

'There are not only too many rules, which take a very long time to change, there are too many committees, too many people who go on too long – they go on well into their seventies. Football is a young man's sport. If you're sixty-five and you become a Life President, or whatever, you move upstairs and if you've served the FA well, then no one should stop you going to a Cup Final, but you shouldn't be running the game. It's a changing world, a changing game and rules have to change, too.'

To those outside football it often seems that things change regardless of the FA or even in spite of the Association's efforts.

'It's got to be like that, because the FA and the Football League have got no charisma, have they? Unfortunately, they have not employed the right people or paid high enough wages, so they haven't really taken the game by the scruff of the neck to stop the chairmen from doing it. Eventually, the chairmen get frustrated because they're thinking that people are dictating to them who haven't got anything to lose. They're not just lacking in charisma – they're not responsible enough and they're not intelligent enough. So what the chairmen are eventually going to do is to say: "Right! We'll run our own league." It's not surprising that that should be the aim. You'll end up with, say, eight club chairmen and they'll run it as a company. It *should* change. Whether it does or not remains to be seen. It'll take a long time in this country.

'We've got the ridiculous situation here of having the FA running the Premier League and then having the Football League running the rest – two separate bodies. We've got different rules, different kick-off dates . . . it's all ego, really. It's just bloody nonsense. Football should be run by one body and that's the end of it. Unfortunately we've had two bodies for a hundred-odd years and it'll carry on like that until the clubs decide: "Bugger you lot! We're pulling away." '

Certainly if chairmen want to challenge the FA on anything, the smart money is seldom going to be on the mob from Lancaster Gate. Alan Sugar had little trouble getting the FA to give Spurs back points that had been deducted as a punishment for disregarding some of its rules, when he brought in his legal experts to challenge the Association's actions. The Football Association ended up revealing about as much bottle as a Temperance Society tea party. Many professional bodies lack teeth. With the FA, even its gums seem in a bad state of repair. Back to Dave Bassett:

'Their rules can't stand up in court, they haven't moved forward with the times and it's their own fault because they haven't allowed top people in to take a look at things. Twenty years ago, they should have had somebody of good intelligence and knowledge to come in and reorganise everything.

'Football's got to move forward and eventually the changes will come. We can see now that chairmen are getting frustrated. They're contributing a lot of money to their clubs, and they don't want to be dictated to. They want to lay down the rules of what can be done and not stick with the rules of fifty years ago or a hundred years ago or twenty years ago. Life has to move on. Things are currently ridiculous, with the League and the FA pulling in different directions and not being able to agree on anything. What happens in Italy? There's one federation! Germany? One federation. Brazil? The same. There are too many people with too many egos. It's jobs for the old boys. Committee after committee. They're all part-time so it takes ages to get anything changed. The amount of procedure involved is enormous.

'The chairmen are thinking that they don't have to put up with all this and I don't know whether it'll happen, but I can see them perhaps pulling away from the FA. There's this thing now that UEFA will only recognise the Football Association for European cups. Well, if the Premier League clubs pull out, and everybody's gone and the FA hasn't got any teams, we might get banned from Europe for a couple of years but then eventually the Barcelonas and the Inter Milans will want the Man Uniteds back. It's big money. They're not going to say: "We're going to ban you because you've pulled away from the FA and set up your own football federation"!

'The way they dealt with the Inter-Toto Cup was inept. [Spurs and Wimbledon feeling forced to play whether they liked it or not, the FA having promised that three British clubs would take part, and then being accused of fielding under-strength sides and punished by UEFA. The punishment was later overturned. Strangely, Sheffield Wednesday were not accused of fielding an under-strength side, something the club should complain about most vigorously in my view.] The way they dealt last season with Cantona, Paul Merson, Chris Armstrong and Alan Sugar was all inept. There was the over-reaction over the Hillsborough tragedy, forcing everyone to sit down and then deciding that that may not have been the best idea after all . . . some poor thinking all round.'

So there we are. The only sense in which the FA really seem to be in charge is that, if chairmen can give managers a headache, so the FA can still give chairmen a headache. But for how much longer? It can only be a matter of time before the most powerful voices in the game (and, alas, as in any other game, money talks) decide to go their own way and do their own thing. Fortunately for traditionalists, the fact that they all seem to hate one another with a vengeance may slow the process down a little.

It's unlikely to be held back for ever, though, and with a governing body that, like the old Soviet politburo, seeming to be in severe danger of all its members dying at once, change will have to come one of these days.

8: Night of the Minnow

'Size isn't important.'

Claire Rayner

Rather like the Kennedy assassination, everyone remembers what they were doing when they heard about it.

For my part, I had just come back from the West Country, having watched in wonder as Newcastle demolished Bristol City 5–0 in the Coca-Cola Cup. I was actually in *Manchester* at the time. 'It's nothing to shout about,' Manchester United supporters had maintained. 'They're only a Second Division side.'

And then, later that evening, it happened. York City beat the Reds 3–0 at Old Trafford. Joy of joys! The Red Machine out of the Coca-Cola Cup (they nearly reprieved themselves on the away leg, but not quite)! It *is* the Real Thing.

Naturally, the Red Devils found ways of explaining it to themselves ('We never wanted to be in the Coca-Cola Cup, anyway. Poxy little tournament!') and it probably wasn't as big a shock to the system as getting knocked out of Europe on away goals that same week. But for those who do not support Man U – and there are still one or two about – it was sheer bliss. The *schadenfreude* that every supporter can't help but feel came straight to the surface. Sure, the FA Cup would throw up other giant killers (Hitchin, Stevenage, Canvey Island . . .) but none could match this result for sheer hilariousness. I'm sorry if there are any Manchester United supporters reading this who don't appreciate these sentiments, but look at it from anyone else's point of view and you'll appreciate the feeling.

Giant killings happen every season. They are as inevitable as price increases, torrential rain on a match day and Eric Hall appearing on television. For supporters of big sides like Newcastle (and, of course, Man U), they are no fun at all. For those who support clubs like York City, they bring pleasure of near-orgasmic intensity. In fact, it was not so many years ago that York had rubbed Arsenal's noses in it, too. Imagine! A club that has humiliated Arsenal and Manchester United! They should get some sort of special award.

But how does it feel to be a giant killer or a giant killed from the point of view of the David or Goliath in the manager's seat?

To begin to answer that question, it is important to appreciate just how huge the gulf is between the Premier League and the rest of the football league, currently sponsored by Endsleigh Insurance. A large satellite TV deal struck mid-season may narrow that gap, but, for the time being, it's like chalk and not so much cheese as some kind of hugely expensive high-tech computerised multi-media communication facility. And the chalk's worn down to the last inch.

All the same, there are times when small can be beautiful. One man amply qualified to talk about it is Alan Smith, former manager of Crystal Palace, itself a club known to indulge in a spot of giant killing. The size of the giant is relative, though, and, following a fiercely fought, soul-destroying battle against relegation from the Premier League, and a marked deterioration in the relationship with his chairman, Ron Noades (a relationship which hadn't exactly been hot to start with), he moved to Wycombe Wanderers, a Second Division club very much on a par with York City. By the middle of the season, his new club were in the upper reaches of their division, being tipped as candidates for promotion. (Alan's greatest success was bringing Palace straight back up into the Premier League, following earlier relegation under previous manager Steve Coppell, in his first season as manager there. Coppell returned to Palace as Smith's replacement.)

Just how different is it, being with a smaller club?

'It's very different. It isn't so pressurised. I spent two years as the manager of Palace and first of all I had a chairman who I think was basically jealous of me [Smith's separate business interests had put him in a better financial position than most managers and, it was rumoured, not far off the chairman himself – maybe better!], whereas I haven't got that any more. I haven't got the problems with agents that I had. Every player at Palace had an agent. One had four or five. I found the players at Palace were much more streetwise, but, of course, they were earning such incredible money. The lowest-paid player I had at Palace was on twenty-five thousand a year. I had a lot of players on a hundred thousand a year and I had a few on two hundred and fifty thousand pounds a year. Now, their perception of life is totally different to that of the guys at Wycombe, and lastly, there was the media attention. I mean, I happened to be at a club that got promoted as First Division champions. We got about the same number of points as Newcastle got when they were promoted the year before. They got about ninety-eight. I think we got about ninety-four. Forest were promoted from the same division as us and we were eight or nine points clear of them and then the following year, Middlesbrough, whom we'd beaten in the last game of the season to go up as champions, went up with less points than us. Look where all those teams have gone. Look where Newcastle have gone, where Forest and Middlesbrough have gone . . . and look where Palace have gone [at the time of the interview, they were in the bottom half of the First Division and fading fast]! It's interesting. I've got a Palace team photograph up there. It was taken in 1993–94, my first year as a manager, at the start of the season. In that picture of thirty-six people, there are only four left. That's an incredible turnover, isn't it? And I think, of those four, by the end of this month, there'll only be two! And they're all with good clubs. A lot of those guys in that picture are now with top clubs.

'So there was all that. Then, in my second year as manager, there was a lot of media hype. There was the Chris Armstrong drugs thing, the Cantona thing – he was sent off at our ground. Somehow the Noades–Smith thing caught the imagination of the press when they didn't have anything to write about, so they'd dig it up or try and come up with something. There were a lot of those things.

'In the five months I've been at Wycombe, I haven't had a problem with the chairman. I suspect I won't. He seems a straight sort of guy, not quite so egoistic, and it's run by a committee there. You don't have the trouble with the agents or all that media attention.'

When you look at it that way, the move to Wycombe Wanderers doesn't seem half bad. And then there's all that opportunity for giant killing. Unfortunately, at the time of the interview, Wycombe had just been knocked out of the FA Cup by Gillingham on a replay. Defeat is no easier for the minnows than for the Man U's:

'I find all of the defeats very hard to accept. With a defeat, you can't do anything about it. It's done, it's dusted and it's over. Losing to Gillingham left an aftermath. I can't get it out of my system. Logically, without being big-headed, I should be able to come home and think: "Well, I've got a nice house, I don't owe anything, I haven't got any debts. So what?" But I don't. I'm forty-nine in December and I'm thinking: "Shit! We've lost a game and we're out of the FA Cup for this year!

Terrible!" But it isn't. There's life after that. Yet I find it very difficult to find that life.'

Not surprising! The previous season, despite Palace's relegation, Smith had taken them to the FA Cup semi-finals and previously, before he became a full-time manager, Palace had gone further still. Is it the case, as is often claimed, that players can 'lift themselves' to perform better in cup competitions than throughout the season in the league?

'There is no doubt that a psychological situation exists, but I've got to say that those players are under-achievers, most of them. If they have to do it for cup games, but can't do it week-in-week-out, then I haven't got much time for them. I mean, in my life, I've tended to be a bit of a week-in-week-out person. I haven't had particular highs in my life and I haven't had particular lows, thank God, in anything. I tend to put out fifty-two weeks of the year on pretty much a level and I like those types of people around me.'

This sense of moderation and keeping things in perspective is very like that echoed by Walter Smith in an earlier chapter. Perhaps they *are* related.

'It's weird. I went to an FA Cup final with Palace when we played Man U, as the assistant manager. There's a photo over there of me on the pitch in the semi-final, when we beat Liverpool. I really didn't take it as a particular high. It's funny now, looking back. I just did it as a job. I never, ever thought I'd go to a Cup Final and sit on the bench, hear the band. But it *became* a job. I hate to say that. It did become a job. I had to deal with Eric Hall, who was agent to some of our players, and Paul [Stretford, another agent]. I had to deal with the media, as assistant manager. Steve [Coppell] didn't want to deal with it. The relationship was good that day, but Steve wasn't really very interested in that side of it. So it became a job and I just got on with it – and then, two weeks later, I thought: "Christ! I've been to a Cup Final! Did it really happen?" It's not like I thought it was going to be, thinking it was really terrific. It became a job. But that's probably my personality.'

So being there at Wembley as the all-conquering underdogs isn't always what we think it's going to be like. Of course, Palace lost in that final, but one club that really did go all the way was Wimbledon, beating Liverpool to the trophy in 1988.

When Joe Kinnear took over as manager from Bobby Gould, that achievement was already enshrined in the side's history. But as Joe pointed out, the atmosphere at a smaller club can be different in many ways from that of a large one. It's more intimate, more personal, more *friendly*.

'I like characters. I like players who express themselves, as long as they've got a serious nature to them. I think there's got to be a happy medium where you don't go overboard. You have to give players a little bit of licence, but you've got to let them know who the boss is, so they respect it. I don't know what it is about this club. I had twelve years at Spurs and never felt the warmth of character that there is at this club. We had a great time at Tottenham, played in numerous Cup Finals, won them all, did this that and the other, because we had great players. But I don't think we socialised enough. I think that bonding is what makes this club very special and it's something we need and encourage. The players look after each other at this club. There's no breakaway factions. Everybody's in the same boat. We don't have any stars here, though some players go on to fulfil that role themselves. I think all the good 'uns we've had, according to the feedback we've had at this club, are very popular at the clubs they join and the first thing they're quizzed on is: "How do they do it at Wimbledon?" . . . I've bumped into Dennis Wise; John Scales came back here during the break . . . When players leave us for other clubs, the door has never been shut on them, they're always welcome back. John Scales said he'd never worked so hard as when he'd been here – he's finding training much easier at Liverpool!

'When you look at bigger clubs, and managers buy players for whom they pay astronomical amounts of money, they tend to take them for granted and feel that they're buying the finished article. It's: "Come in here, we'll keep you ticking over, play a game of five-a-side and then go out there and produce – 'cos if you do it, we'll replay you." I've always been of the opinion that players need specific training. If I see a player like Warren Barton, I think: "He can be the best, so let's make him the best." Let's get it into his head that three afternoons a week, he's got to practise, to work on his touch or whatever, to build on strengths and become stronger with the ultimate goal of being the best player and going on to play for your country. I said the same about Dean Holdsworth when I bought him. I said: "This kid's going to score goals, he's two-footed, but we mustn't take that for granted." And when we come to sell him on to a bigger club, he'll be the finished article. But the nice thing about our players is that they do work to improve themselves. Dean will want to do what Warren did. They all want to play for Liverpool or Man United, and always have that in mind. So, as long as I can motivate them, and get the best out of them on a daily basis, then they'll continuously improve, year in, year out. We can't afford to let standards drop, I preach that to the players: "If you really want to achieve, you've got to work for it. It doesn't come from nothing."

'Our strength now will spring from having the right

structure at youth team level. We've got thirteen players in the first-team squad who are home-grown. They're all good players.'

Newcastle chairman Sir John Hall has said that he would like an all-Geordie side playing for United. Realistically, that isn't going to happen as long as the club is in a position to buy in better players from elsewhere. There have been periods when large sections of sides like Liverpool or Manchester United weren't even *English*, let alone from anywhere near the Lancashire area. Conversely, there was a time when a large group of English players popped across the border to play for Rangers.

Kinnear explained his approach to structuring the youth team:

'We could field a side of players all from Wimbledon. We've signed another five from the youth team this year. They'd had a tremendous run, but that's a hell of a lot of players when you consider the squad numbers. Now I've got what I consider a top twenty-four players and I keep a further twenty promising youngsters, so there are two factions, depending on how I cut the youngsters. I probably keep more youth players on than any other club, but I think it's the case that we really believe these players could save us fortunes in the long term. We always take three or four of them with us if we go away. If it's somewhere like Newcastle, I'll bring six. They become part of it. They're there in the dressing room. It gives them an idea of how it works. I make sure that from the first day they sign professional forms, they're treated with the same respect that a character like Vinnie Jones is – or any of the senior pros. We gel very well. The kids love it here, they enjoy being here and they stay here. We haven't lost one kid, I think, in the last six years. There are lots of new kids coming through, all promising kids from the last five years, and it's saved a fortune on the transfer market, so the system has more than paid its way.

'When I bump into Dennis Wise now, he says it was one of the best times of his career, while he was here. It taught him everything. He would come back every afternoon just to take free kicks and corner kicks all on his own. I bet he doesn't do that now he's at Chelsea.'

No, but I bet he spends more time with faith healers if Glenn Hoddle practises what he preaches.

'The wonderful thing about Wimbledon,' Joe continued, 'is that our players are very adaptable, and they believe in what I do and they believe in us winning matches. And if, tactically, we outthink opposition and outwork them, well, it's in the rules. If I say to Vinnie, mark Gascoigne out of the game, well, it gets us the result we're looking for on the day. I get fed up at times with other managers whinging after we've won games.'

It's not a bad position to be in, the minnow that's envied by the whales.

'Last season, we beat Blackburn four–two, we beat Manchester United up at Old Trafford . . .'

I have some vague recollection that Newcastle may have fallen to the Dons as well, but I seem to have developed a mental block on all memories of that day.

'Sometimes some managers will make cheap comments and say things like: "Well, they are what they are and I'll say no more." Well, I could say the same, but I tend to bite my tongue. I could say: "Have a closer look at some of your own players." '

Still, perhaps such sneering should really be seen as a back-handed compliment. 'I am what I am' worked for Popeye, and he had a reputation for making mincemeat of larger opponents, too. I think it was Danny Blanchflower who once said that the best side *always* wins. Everything else is just rumour.

But how does it feel to be Goliath vanquished? To know that, we have to go right to the top again. Walter Smith knew that Rangers were not going to do as well in Europe as many of their fans thought, that prior success had been giant killing on *their* part rather than the establishment of some new status quo. Yet surely in Scottish league matches, *anyone* who beats Rangers can be marked down as a giant killer. Has anyone ever thought about what it's like to be the giant?

> 'To retain your success is very, very difficult. When I was assistant manager here, I was able to observe international players at work and find out how they reacted and how they wanted to be treated in a way that would get the best out of them. That was something I picked up in the five years between leaving Dundee United and taking over as manager of Rangers.'

That would indeed have helped. It would have meant that his style upon taking over would not have been too stark a contrast to that of his predecessor, Graeme Souness. For Souness, taking over at Liverpool following the shock departure of Kenny Dalglish, who claimed he wanted to take time out of the game because of the stress associated with it, it was a nightmare move. In fact, Liverpool FC was looking like something of a minnow itself, by the time he left.

'I think the two situations were different,' said Smith.

> 'When he took over at Rangers, the club hadn't won a league championship for nine seasons, so it was obvious that he had to come in and change the playing staff. He was able to do that fairly easily, because no one at the club had been successful. It was easy to bring in Chris Woods and Terry Butcher and Graeme Souness himself, and that picked everybody up, gave them a lift. That was how he initially started at Rangers and that gave him a springboard to go on. With Liverpool, it was a totally different set of circumstances. They had what they felt

there was a team that had been *very* successful, but were getting older and had to be changed round. Now, there are a great many more difficulties in doing that.

'I wouldn't like to comment on what went on, because I wasn't there – I mean, I speak to Graeme a lot, but I was never privy to what was going on there – but the two sets of circumstances were very different when he started at the two clubs. It's a problem, though, in managing all football teams. Whenever you take over at a club, you're under the microscope. When I took over from him at Rangers, we had a couple of wee hiccups and then a long period of success at the club – I'm not saying that was all due to me! – but when you come to the end of that, people start to question every decision you make and then you have to start again. If another manager comes in, he has to change it round again and so it goes on.'

So how much pressure is there on a giant like the Gers not to capitulate to a giant killer under any circumstances? And how difficult is it living up to what, realistically, is an impossible ideal (no side can ever win *everything*)?

'Looking at that, you know, I don't think people fully appreciate how difficult it is. OK, they can look at us and say that we buy in a better standard of player, but that's like saying: "Give someone plenty of money and they'll win anything." There's a lot more that goes into it besides buying players. That's one of the things I think people take for granted all the time. At the start of every season now the view is: "There's nobody that can beat Rangers." That's everybody's viewpoint. Rangers can never encounter a difficulty. They can never encounter any obstacle that will prevent them from winning the league championship. That's hard to live up to.'

And when someone does break through the armour?

> 'It's difficult to overcome. There was a bit of last season when we lost to Celtic, we lost to AEK Athens in the European Cup and we lost to Falkirk in the League Cup at Ibrox. So, getting knocked out of two cup competitions and getting beaten by your oldest rivals was very difficult, probably my hardest period since I came to Rangers. It had an effect on us. There's no doubt that we took a knock in confidence. We had a lot going on around the club at that time, a lot of injury problems. I'm never one to highlight an injury problem, but I felt at that stage that I had to use it in the dressing room – not in front of the press but within the dressing room – and I tried to use it at that time to make sure that players retained their confidence, that it didn't knock us too much. Fortunately, we did get over it, but it did take us a while to do so. But I think these problems occur at all football clubs.'

That's probably true. It's all relative, after all. Wycombe Wanderers are minnows compared to Crystal Palace who are minnows compared to Manchester United. Even clubs like Rangers and Manchester United have been humbled by European opponents. And when you do get to the top, it's no fun. At Barcelona, if you have four defeats on the trot, the chances are you'll get the boot. Perhaps many players – and managers, too – fail to appreciate the advantages of being a small club: the warmth; the camaraderie; the hope without the pressure.

After all, Stan Collymore, despite a dramatic improvement in his form at Liverpool as the season progressed, was probably at his best – and happiest – playing for Southend. And Matt Le Tissier looks as though he'll never leave Southampton. In the end, there is no romance left if you've ceased to become the giant killer and are now part of the giant.

9: Out on a Limb

'There's none more lost than them that don't know where they're going.'

Bob Paisley

For those who want to produce an artistic work about football, say a novel, a film or a play, there can be few more engaging or romantic figures than the great football maverick, the outsider. He stands alone from the rest of the team. He makes his own decisions. He won't have others running his life for him and telling him what to do. And through it all, where there is doubt, he'll chew it up and spit it out. He'll face it all and he'll stand tall and he'll do it his way.

There is also a sentiment among some fans (and, let's face it, we fans can be a pretty sentimental bunch) that football is already an art form. Allied to this belief is the unshakeable conviction that poetry wins matches. Not *actual* poetry of the sort Eric Cantona apparently claims to enjoy reading in his spare time – that would clearly be ridiculous – but the metaphorical poetry created by a footballer of Cantona's calibre playing at his most graceful and balletic. We all have our treasured memories when we saw a match that wasn't a mere ninety minutes of slog and graft but was like a great work of imagination and artistry, crafted by the hand of some footballing god, bigger than the players, bigger than the manager, bigger than even the chairman in all his glory. I'm no different. I'll treasure the memory of Paul Gascoigne's first hat trick for Spurs (two of the goals coming from audacious free kicks, one curling majestically past Shilton into the top left-hand corner of the net, the other no less majestically into the top *right*-hand corner) for ever. I'd like to believe in my heart of hearts that poetry wins matches.

But it doesn't.

Or at least it needn't. There are plenty of things a shrewd manager can substitute for artistry and poetry. Frankly, if it was only poetry that won matches, Arsenal would never have won the Championship. Not even once.

And it's not just that poetry doesn't always win matches. It can be argued quite strongly that overdoing the poetry can even *lose* you matches. Flair is all very well, but how many times is it just a euphemism for inconsistency? We can all look back at the fancy-dans of yesteryear who didn't get as many games, particularly at the highest level, as their talent might suggest they should. But it's quite possible that they were overlooked because their individual brilliance got in the way of the team doing well collectively. Managers like Bob Paisley knew that temperament was as important as natural skill, possibly more so. It can be exasperating to the onlooker if a talented player is left out of a side at the expense of someone who has noticeably less panache but 'fits in better with how the team play'. Yet I suspect that such decisions have been made since the game began and are made outside the game in offices and factories on a daily basis.

Of course, managers like to get a reputation for producing sides that *play football*, that is to say, play with style and elegance and *je ne sais quoi*. Give the fans something a little bit special. Some sides manage it: Brazil in the seventies; Liverpool, under Paisley and Shankly, in the seventies and eighties; dare I suggest a side like Newcastle United at the moment, when they are playing at their best? But these are rare examples. Far more often, it is boringly consistent, workmanlike sides who clean up in the hunt for trophies. The Germans have been very successful internationally, but certainly haven't always been entertaining to watch. And can anyone really say that, in winning the 1994–95 League Championship, Blackburn impressed everyone with their grace and artistry?

If it's true that you can win and leave out all the beauty of Pele's 'beautiful game', is it also true that artistry can backfire? Perhaps in the modern game this is especially so. As Czech goalkeeper Ivo Victor, whose side won the 1976 European Championships and who has memories of facing Pele, put it in one interview: 'You will not find a star like Pele today. The game now does not produce individuals like him. Even the good individuals have to be more part of a team. I'm not saying that's a bad thing, just that the game is different today.'

All of which suggests that managers may not always take the same starry-eyed view of today's effortlessly talented players as the fans do. What do they make of the likes of Stan Collymore, so successful at Southend, yet so isolated from players at Nottingham Forest that on occasion they wouldn't celebrate with him after he had scored a goal? In signing for Liverpool at the beginning of the season in an eight-and-a-half million pound deal, Collymore became the most expensive player in the country, but remains something of an enigma. The jury is still out on just how good he really is, and I doubt many would describe him as a bargain. Or what about Graeme Le Saux, an undeniably talented player who nevertheless ended up fighting with his own team-mate, David Batty, during a widely televised European Cup match? And what of Matt Le Tissier?

To some, the Southampton midfielder is a genius, even, in their eyes, the best player in the country. Certainly some of the goals he has scored, particularly from dead-ball situations, have been little short of magical. On the other hand, those who don't spend week in, week out watching Le Tissier at The Dell do tend to see only the best bits. He has a reputation for being lazy, for not being hungry enough for success. While his continued non-selection for the England squad caused consternation in some sections of the media, a loss of form early in the season led many to re-evaluate his contribution and decide that perhaps he wasn't that great after all. All geniuses go through bad patches, his defenders would argue. Indulge them. Give them a free role. Build the team around them. Watch them shine.

It's easy to forget that football is a team game. The media always like to focus on the stars, to bring out the individuals in the game and write about them. Agents also tend to encourage individuality, rather than the collective greater good that clubs might prefer. But we're not talking about sports like golf and tennis, where you're on your own and the cult of the individual is therefore everything. Nor are we talking about the media world from which many of Le Tissier's fiercest supporters spring, where mercurial talent will get you far and where one person, if they shine brightly enough, can get their own show. On Planet Football everyone has to play together and get on well, at least while they're on the pitch.

To be fair to Le Tissier, he hasn't had much chance to prove that he can go beyond the status of maverick and fully integrate himself into a team. The Southampton side are so mediocre that they tend to adapt to him. In many people's eyes, he doesn't just exemplify the team, he *is* the team. Thus, when he plays badly, the team plays badly and given that there are another ten spare players around who occasionally make some sort of contribution, even when he plays well, the team can play badly. Southampton were in trouble all season, Le Tiss or no Le Tiss. So were Manchester City, despite the breathtaking talent of Georgi Kinkladze.

Psychological profiling of players, with which I was involved together with colleague Stephen Smith, suggests that, for the most part, managers in this country would rather have a fit, athletic player without too many ideas of his own than someone more creative but less of a grafter in their team. This may sound depressing to fans, but the feeling seems to be that while one supremely talented player may be an expensive luxury you can just about afford, two become a liability.

I asked Joe Kinnear whether this was an accurate interpretation of many managers' views.

> 'I think there's very much a case for these talented players, but within the team circle, in the framework of the game. I don't think you can ask players to do things they're not capable of doing. I'd never ask any player at Wimbledon to do something which I don't believe they are capable of doing. I know what Vinnie's capabilities are, I know what his strengths are. Therefore, he'll come along and he'll play to his strengths. I know that if Vinnie's playing in the middle of the park, then I need somebody quicker alongside him to get forward and to support the front two, somebody like Oyvind Leonhardsen, a Norwegian who's like lightning, very pacy, a lovely player up and down. He scores goals and blends in nicely with Vinnie. Robbie Earle is another one – box to box, very effective. So, I think it's knowing your players and if you've got ten players out on the pitch, you still need somebody that is gifted and is going to win the game for you. Now, if you've got a Matthew Le Tissier, then you'll almost certainly be saying, "Go and win the game for us, Matt! You go and have a free role *but* within the set-up. These are the areas we'd like you to turn up eventually . . . if you haven't got anything better to do, that is!" Well, he's not much as far as work rate is concerned!
>
> 'There *is* a place for these talented players, but I don't think that, to be successful, you can have too many of them. There's got to be labourers and artists. A team full of Matt Le Tissiers could never work. Ardiles tried to do that at Tottenham and his motto was: "Let's get beat eight-six every week!" I don't think there are too many managers in football who actually believe that. He must be the exception. But people have got to

remember that we're in a professional business and it's just that. I know people say we're here to entertain, and this that and the other, but if you look at your teams you'll have, say, Manchester United. Yes, it's the "Theatre of Dreams", but they also have to go away and graft and get results. They work extremely hard. They have to go long in some games and hit it over the top to a winger. When that happens, people will say "It's a wonderful pass." If Wimbledon do it, it's a "long ball". I'm always trying to take journalists to task over this. One day I read a report about us and it was all "long ball, long ball, long ball" and on the same page there was a report about Matt Le Tissier and they said he'd done a beautiful sixty-yard pass over the top. Now, Vinnie Jones had been hitting sixty-yard balls all day for Dean Holdsworth to get on the end of, but when Matt Le Tissier does it, it's described as something wonderful, as though no one else in football can do this. And often he'll do that a couple of times and those are the only two incidents in the whole game, but that's what you'll see when Sky show the clips from the match.'

Stan Collymore has certain parallels with Le Tissier. Like him, he shone at a seaside club, Southend, in a team which was at the time so mediocre by comparison that none but die-hard fans of that club can so much as name them. Unlike his Southampton equivalent, he chose to move on to a much bigger club, Nottingham Forest (the kind of move Le Tissier seems very deliberately to have avoided). He then went even bigger, in fact breaking domestic transfer records with his move to Liverpool. His move from Forest was far from smooth and far from good-tempered, masterminded as it was by Paul Stretford, the agent who had represented Andy Cole in his transfer from Newcastle to Manchester United. In the wake of that transfer, Cole had not regained his goal-scoring touch to anything like the extent he had possessed at his former club. Everyone wondered whether the same would happen to 'Stan the Man', especially after he implied criticism of his new manager in a widely quoted magazine interview, accusing him of spending a fortune on a commodity without spending too much time thinking how he was going to use it.

Hot stuff! What did managers make of it? Well, Collymore had certainly not been a target for Joe Kinnear in the days when he was younger and cheaper: 'He's got a lot to live up to. At the time he first went to Southend, I spoke to coaches at Crystal Palace who had sold him and they seriously wondered whether he was intelligent enough to play in Premier League football. It'll be interesting to see what happens to him.'

One person who knows all about Stan Collymore is Alan Smith. It was largely on his recommendation that Palace sold him to Southend for next to nothing in the first place, since Smith believed he'd never cut the mustard as a top pro. Fingers could point to Smith, accompanied by the accusation that he had made a terrible mistake in letting a player of Collymore's talent go. He is largely unrepentant, however. He smiles wryly about it.

'Yes, I overlooked Stan Collymore. Amongst the many players I helped develop, who have moved on to bigger and better clubs, he was the one I let go. People could indeed accuse me of that.'

But he is still unconvinced that Collymore will live up to his billing. 'I wouldn't pay money to go and watch Stan Collymore,' he said. 'I'd pay to watch Shirley Bassey. She's got real, undisputed talent. But not Stan. I think he is a guy who cannot find himself, he's lost in a mist of his own mind. I don't think we know who the real Stan Collymore is and I don't think he knows.'

What about his reputation for disliking training and hard physical exercise generally, something he freely admits?

> 'I don't understand that. I think for most managers and players, certainly for me, the most enjoyable thing is training. It's enjoyable, you're out in the fresh air, it's only for two hours a day, there is no pressure in it – if you're healthy. I don't see

any hardship in it, personally. He saw it as a hardship. He looked on training as a punishment.

'I think anyone who earns twelve thousand pounds a week, which is *phenomenal* money – I never earned anything like that in my life, *ever*, anywhere *near* – some of the comments he comes out with ["I'd rather be somewhere else on six thousand pounds a week"] border on . . . well, it doesn't even deserve comment. Pathetic!'

This factor has probably contributed to Collymore's being cast even more in the role of outsider. It is not only considerably more than many of his team-mates earn, it's more than his manager earns, too.

Is Collymore perhaps just bearing the burden of being an individual? This is something which is often brought up about another player, Graeme Le Saux. He appears to enjoy his reputation for being a bit of an oddball, having unusual interests and taking a different view of life from most footballers. He's probably relaxed about his separateness from the rest of the team. At Chelsea, he once tore off his shirt and threw it away upon being substituted, not the hallmark of someone who places team spirit uppermost on his agenda.

This all came to a head during Blackburn's dismal performance in Europe, when a fight broke out between Le Saux and his own team-mate, David Batty. Altercations like this are indicative of team disharmony in the extreme, living illustrations of a side tearing itself apart. Both European performance and early-season league form had been appalling for Blackburn, the previous season's champions. So, was Le Saux being victimised for not being 'one of the lads', for daring to resist succumbing to a collective mentality, something guaranteed at least to win him a few friends in the media? And isn't the same true of Stan Collymore – isn't he just daring to be different, to be an individual? Alan Smith gave his response:

'I don't think Stan is an individual. I think he is a run-of-the-mill, ordinary guy who happens to have struck relatively lucky. I think Le Saux *is* different. He wants to read the *Independent* or the *Guardian*, he wants to go round antique shops. He's not the norm. Mark Bright was very much like that. Mark was different, he didn't want to be one of the boys, and if you are slightly different, then you do get picked out. I don't think Stan was picked out for that reason. Le Saux is not the norm of the average professional footballer but I think a lot of European footballers are like that.'

Did somebody mention Cantona?

'Stan couldn't be in Europe. He couldn't play for an Italian club or a German club. But I suspect Le Saux could, because he would be a bit more disciplined. Bright would have been able to have done so. I think, as a manager, you've got to accept that there are some people who are different. You can't get at a guy because he reads a book or doesn't want to do what normal guys do. I think that with Stan it's different. You've hit the nail on the head, with him telling us that he didn't like training. It's ludicrous for a young man to be talking like that when you know that that is an expected part of the job.

'That's why man-management in football is quite difficult, though. You are normally dealing with a lot of different egos. I mean, even at a club like Wycombe, I've got twenty-four professionals. I've got eleven apprentices. You're not going to be loved by all of those. At any one time it means that fifty per cent of your workforce could be against you. You'll certainly have fifty per cent of your workforce that don't agree with what you're doing. It would be very unusual in business that the manager of a factory or of an office would have fifty per cent of the workforce against them.'

I'm not so sure. Ask anyone who used to work for Robert Maxwell, and the figure was probably nearer one hundred per cent!

> 'It *is* a team game, though. I think there are certain criteria that have to be accepted by everyone. Everybody has got to wear the same kit, they've got to be there on time and should travel on the team coach unless it's obviously not practical to do so. It is a team game, and I think there are certain things you must do to conform and if you don't, like anything in society, it will cause resentment and it will set you out, won't it? The press love to write about players like Le Tissier because they are different and it's better to write about something different, but sitting here today, by coincidence, Southampton lost two–one last night to Reading, ending their Coca-Cola Cup run, and Matt Le Tissier didn't do anything. He lets you down, I suspect, more times than he gets you out of the mire.'

The assertion that flair players are automatically more difficult to manage is refuted by Tommy Burns. Celtic have always had a reputation for playing creative, passing, positive football. However, he agrees with Alan Smith that such players might do better on the continent. Does independence equate with stroppiness?

> 'I don't think it's always the case. There have been flair players in recent years who have been difficult to manage, but that doesn't apply to some of the best players in Europe. They're free-spirited, they like to *play* the game and there's no problem with that so long as you can let them know what their role is within the team without chaining them down or tying them down in any way. The ball should be passed about, but at the same time, it should be passed about with a purpose. If the other team hasn't got the ball, they can't score a goal, but at the same time, when you knock the ball about, players have got to be sharp, they've got to be alert and know that

someone can make their own run somewhere and all of a sudden you've got a chance of getting a goal. You're in behind them, or over the top of them or you're off to the side or whatever and it's a question of concentrating where to position the ball and where not to position the ball.'

Was there a difference in the style of football encouraged at Kilmarnock from that at Celtic?

'At Kilmarnock, we were in a position of having many players whose ability level was very limited, but with big hearts and a determination to work hard and make it difficult for teams to play against us, so we'd operate that system. At Celtic, we have a lot of international players, so you have to look a bit closer at teamwork but expect to see more passing of the ball.'

Is this excessive diplomacy? Perhaps not. After all, players can be talented and play an effective passing game without all being mercurial individuals, determined to do their own thing. Perhaps when we look at those successful Liverpool sides of the seventies and eighties, we miss the discipline and the fact that individualism gave way to a collective mentality, the greater good of the team, and all we see is the beauty of that one-touch passing. Tommy Burns seemed to be encouraging that at Celtic with some success if the results were anything to go by. The team was slowly closing in on Rangers. The customary one-horse race was becoming a two-horse race.

But it doesn't always run smoothly, as Dave Bassett admits:

'Being realistic, the fans don't always know what's going on behind the scenes. There are always going to be times when a player may become a disruptive influence on the team and can unsettle the side. This can get in the way of team spirit.

Sometimes a player gets into a "comfort zone" where he's reached a plateau, is happy with what he's earning, thinks his place in the team is automatic and just stops trying. He doesn't want to push himself any more and he can't get by on just talent alone. In those situations, when you've talked to the player and you still can't get a response, you sometimes have no option but to sell that player because he's having a negative influence on the team.'

Could Le Tissier be caught inside his little comfort zone? Is that, more than a sense of loyalty to Southampton, what has kept him at the club for so long? Naturally, when you are so much more talented than the players around you, the manager may have no option but to persist in building the team around you, even if your game has gone off the boil. Interestingly, however, Southampton announced that they were trying to experiment with options where Le Tissier's role was less prominent. Could this continue to the point of playing without him?

Perhaps, in a team game, no one is truly indispensable. Often selling a player can weaken a team considerably (Dave Bassett says this was very much true of Brian Deane, whom he was forced to sell at Sheffield United), but teams tend to go on nonetheless. Manchester United are enjoying success long after George Best. The Dutch are still up there without Johan Cruyff. They might not have done it with anything like the same flamboyance as in 1970, but Brazil still won the 1994 World Cup without Pele.

The reality of what a manager sometimes feels he is forced to do came home to me one Saturday early on in the season as I watched Dulwich Hamlet crash out of the qualifying rounds of the FA Cup against Bognor Regis. The score was 4–2 and an early October exit was painful, particularly in a season which showed genuine promise. It came as a shock to the players, as they had been hoping – quite realistically – for a good cup run (in fact, it was the side's performance in the ICIS League that was to be more impressive), and it turned the spotlight on to their goalkeeper, whose errors many players and fans alike felt were instrumental in the poor result obtained.

The team's goalkeeper was undoubtedly one of the side's most individually talented players, with considerable experience playing for other clubs. He had even played in the European Cup Winners' Cup for Limerick City who play in the League of Ireland. One thing he was not, however, was a mixer and he always seemed separate from the rest of the team, even by the standards of goalkeepers, who have a habit of being a little different. He would often make his own way to matches, rather than travel on the team coach, and when he did travel with the others, he tended to sit apart from the rest of the group. Thus, as the coach pulled away from Bognor's ground, he was not physically there to share the grief and the disappointment. Furthermore, he was not there to say, 'Sorry lads, I let you down a bit today.' That's probably all it would have taken, even if it had been followed up by a '. . . but we all made mistakes today' or something of that ilk. But he wasn't there – he deliberately *of his own choice* wasn't there – and, in such situations, talk can often turn to such topics as commitment towards team values and bonding with the rest of the squad and suspicions of those on the outside.

I didn't elicit manager Frank Murphy's views at the time (you've got to pick your moments when you're talking to managers, and this obviously wasn't going to be the best of times). However, his actions spoke louder than words. By the next match, he had bought a new keeper.

It would be naive to say that this was all down to the keeper being an outsider. Obviously, if he had played better, his remoteness wouldn't have mattered. But, when the chips are down, a little bit out on the edge of the team is a dangerous place to be. In the end, raw ability may not be enough. Personality goes a long way.

Goalkeeping at the club didn't take on a miraculous improvement. There were to be bad results later in the season. In fact, Frank

Murphy brought in a third keeper in February. However, the win in the League that came immediately after the Cup defeat, featuring as it did the new keeper's debut, lifted the spirit of the team. They felt they were back on course for success. Looking at it from the outside, the manager's decision seemed an effective one under the circumstances. At that point in time, with no benefit of hindsight, I think many managers would have acted accordingly.

In terms of rights and wrongs, there are no moral absolutes here. The manager has to do what he thinks is best for the team at any time, and what is best for the team may not be best for talented, mercurial individuals. The question of whether a manager would ever pick someone who was less technically gifted in favour of someone who was a better 'team player' is one which can exasperate fans, but I think the answer is often yes. It isn't just a question about football, either. It's going on all the time in the business world. In a team game, the ability to get on with others can come above everything else.

Stan Collymore's performance was to improve as the season went on. In the wake of his criticisms in the magazine article, his manager, Roy Evans, spent a lot of time with him and tried to understand where he was coming from. This evidently met with some success, and his true niche turned out to be not as an out-and-out striker, but in partnership with Robbie Fowler, laying on goals for him more than scoring them himself. That's not to say that he didn't score a few classic goals himself, perhaps most memorably the one that gave Liverpool victory over Newcastle with seconds to spare, a match which many have described as the best they've ever seen, though, as a Newcastle supporter, I beg to differ. Nice build-up, but I didn't like the ending. It might, in fact, have been at that point that Manchester United knew the Championship was theirs, and I'm sure no Liverpool fans would want *that* on their conscience!

At the very highest level, though, Stan the Man continued to disappoint. Picked for England for a few matches, his performance was lacklustre, bordering on the embarrassing, and in the FA Cup Final, he was anonymous. The extent to which Alan Smith was or wasn't mistaken about his potential is yet to be fully demonstrated.

For Graeme Le Saux, things were to go from bad to worse. Following his ruck with David Batty, he was involved in a collision which left his leg badly broken. Despite having scored a superb goal for England against Brazil, and being extremely highly rated by Terry Venables, he was out injured for the rest of the season, and missed the Euro '96 European Championships, where it is likely he would have got a place in the starting line-up.

This time he was a *complete* outsider, but no longer by choice. Being forced to be separate is different from wanting to be a bit separate, and much more demoralising. From being out on a limb by choice to being out with a broken limb by accident must be soul-destroying. (Blackburn, incidentally, carried on without him. In fact, their performance following his forced absence, coincidentally or not, was to get better.)

Indeed, the one time a manager knows instantly that a player has a problem is when that player sustains a serious injury, one which is likely to keep him out of the team for a long time. Here, maintaining motivation is not so much a case of sticks and carrots, but of offering that player some hope that will give him the strength to go on.

Players like Paul Gascoigne and Ian Durrant, who have dragged themselves back from very serious injuries, are certain to have gone through moments when they felt like just giving up. How can a manager help a player in this position find some silver lining to the dark cloud hanging over them?

'It's an issue you have to deal with all the time because every club has its injuries,' pointed out Mark McGhee.

> 'When I took over at Leicester, we had injuries to what were then probably our three best players – Julian Joachim, Steve Walsh and David Speedie. There was a consensus of opinion

at the club that, had the three of them been fit the whole season, the club may not have been relegated from the Premier League. I don't know how true that is, but I don't think it's too far off – we'd certainly have been a lot closer. Those sorts of players, when they're out – and especially if they're your best players – demand attention and have to be kept interested. It's very difficult to do, but it comes down very often to the individual. Players themselves can help by being the types who can keep themselves motivated to push themselves until they get back into shape. Others you have to stand over and almost whip them in order for them to discipline themselves and to get themselves fit again. Fortunately, at the larger clubs, you have a big enough staff to make sure that all that is carefully monitored and kept under control.

'I've been through it myself as a player. I got an ankle injury and I had it looked at, had a bit of surgery done and I thought that it was never going to be right. I had the operation in the summer, and I always remember that, round about the middle of January, I suddenly found running easier, and at that point I saw the light at the end of the tunnel. But before that, I'd had those thoughts that it was all hopeless, which is dangerous to morale, and because of that experience, I always try to remind my physios never to say "Oh, that's a bad one" or "That'll be six months". If possible, I prefer not to give the player too much information at all, and certainly not to make any diagnosis or prognosis too early or too quickly. I would rather shorten the period it's likely to take to recover and if it takes longer, it takes longer. But you must keep giving the players deadlines and keep giving them targets, just to keep them going. Rather than saying "In six months, you're going to be fit", I'd rather say "In two months you'll be doing this, and in three months you'll be doing that . . ." You've got to phrase things positively for the players themselves, and it's important that your physios think like that, too.

'Injured players still come along for training. They are involved in every turn. There are also places we can send them, such as Lilleshall, the FA's training school. There they can receive specialist treatment and specialist training, but the trick is just to keep them feeling involved.'

How outsiders – whether mavericks or those with injuries – are handled is an important and difficult part of football management.

Football can be a cruel, unsentimental game, with little room for poetry. The fans don't always appreciate that. Managers must.

10: A Change is as Good as a Rest

'I didn't get where I am today by changing horses in mid-stream. Neither Mrs C. J. nor I have ever changed horses in mid-stream.'

C. J., *The Fall and Rise of Reginald Perrin*

As the season progressed, two of the managers involved in this book made sudden and, to many, unexpected career changes. Mark McGhee, who had only come to Leicester City halfway through the previous season, seized on the opportunity presented by Graham Taylor's sacking at Wolverhampton Wanderers and was interviewed for Taylor's old job. His assessors were clearly impressed, for he was offered the post. Wolves are a substantially larger club than Leicester, with a historically stronger tradition of success. Nevertheless, at the time of Mark's move, their position was unflattering compared to Leicester's to say the least, with the Foxes on or about the top of the first division for much of the first half of the season, and Wolves very much at the opposite end.

At around the same time, the boardroom insecurity and lack of morale at Sheffield United finally proved too much for Dave Bassett. He felt it was time to go, for himself and probably also for the good of the club, where a fresh face can sometimes work new magic. For a couple of months he was off the managerial merry-go-round, taking a little stroll to the candy-floss stall, or whatever it is you do when you step off that particular machine. Some, Alan Smith among them, feared that perhaps the stress and insecurity had finally taken their toll on 'Harry's' natural buoyancy and that he would pack up football management altogether.

As it was, this didn't happen. A couple of months later, he was back at troubled Crystal Palace, a club whose management and coaching structure appeared, to the untrained eye, to be mysterious to say the least. Steve Coppell had seemed to be in charge, though in some remote kind of way, as was his wont. Evidently, it hadn't been working. New blood was needed. And so began a new chapter in Harry's game.

Had he missed management?

'During that particular period, I didn't actually miss it, because I was only out of it for about seven weeks and I had quite a lot going on in that time. I was doing media work, radio work, et cetera. But it gave me a chance to take stock of things, really, more than anything else. I had a bit of a rest and a break. There obviously comes a time when you want to get back in. If you've been doing something a long time, you reach the point when you want to get back working with players and trying to win games.

'The game certainly can wear you down sometimes, but I think managers just need to be able to take a break, rather than get out of management altogether. The ideal would be if we had two breaks in the season, a summer one and a winter one. That would give everyone a chance to recharge their batteries.'

Coming into a new club, you are suddenly confronted by lots of players who you may know little about, and certainly not have worked with before. Is this inevitably a disadvantage or can it be turned in your favour?

'Sometimes it can be stimulating that you're working with a

load of different players that you don't know. I think that lifts you sometimes. I believe footballers are all very similar, similar types of characters but in different shapes and sizes and with different personalities, but they're usually good types of people. When you're moving to a new club, there is usually a bit of apprehension because you're meeting people that you don't know, and there's usually a bit of "Oh dear – I hope they like me. I hope everything is going to be all right" type of thing, which is understandable. Once you start, though, you find that everybody is quite friendly, and you get on with it.'

With his reputation for getting to know individual players very well, how long can it take to build up a rapport like that at a new club?

'I think that takes time. You start talking to players and finding out a little about them and you see if you can begin building up a relationship from there. But it does take time. It's not the sort of thing that you can do after just one meeting. It's true that I like to get to know individual players and what makes them tick. In fact, I regard it as not so much learning what makes them tick, but earning their respect and vice versa.'

What is it that makes someone want to leave a club in the first place? After all, Dave Bassett had been at Sheffield United for eight years, in one of football's most stable managerial careers. Despite being unmistakably a Londoner through and through, he had achieved considerable popularity with Yorkshiremen not necessarily noted for their love of Cockneys and their foreign ways. He had taken the club to the Premiership, been cruelly relegated with the last kick of a season, and had even taken The Blades to an FA Cup semi-final, the unique Steel City derby against Sheffield Wednesday, which had been played at Wembley Stadium. The romantic appeal of the Sheffield club was enhanced further when it appeared as itself in the film *When Saturday Comes* starring Sean Bean, which hit cinema screens after Bassett had already left. Leaving a club in these circumstances is never going to be easy.

Yet there had been problems from the first kick of the season: a boardroom shake-up; an unfinished stadium; no money for new players. These things must affect a manager.

> 'It does affect you when it goes on for a period of time. In the initial stages, I wouldn't necessarily subscribe to that. It is possible for things to go wrong behind the scenes without affecting the manager that much. But at Sheffield United, it went on too long not to affect the players, the coaching staff, myself and everyone else. It did eventually have a debilitating effect on everybody.'

Naturally, as these things work out, Crystal Palace's first game with Bassett in charge was to be against none other than Sheffield United. In the chapter about superstitions in this book, you'll find his thoughts on the eeriness of that experience, and on how hard it can be to face old friends and colleagues with renewed vigour, as their rival. It wasn't a particularly new experience to him, however. He had been manager of Watford before and, as Sheffield United boss, had faced them some seven times.

The sun smiled on Crystal Palace that day. The sides drew, but that was just a hint of what was to come in a transformed season. For a Londoner like 'Harry', did coming home have particular poignancy?

'No, not particularly. I mean, obviously I am from London, but that wasn't a big factor in my decision. I had some very happy years at Sheffield United. Players are very similar everywhere.'

Too much is made of the North-South divide, sometimes. The gap between Yorkshire and South London is mainly in the mind. But what of different parts of the Midlands?

Mark McGhee's move to Wolverhampton Wanderers at first looked every bit as successful as Bassett's. A new manager certainly seemed to galvanise the performances of the side, though, as the season progressed, the magic seemed to fade slightly. While the club had certainly escaped relegation into the Second Division, a prospect that was looking imminent under previous manager, Graham Taylor, it finished in the lower half of the First Division, not nearly as far above the relegation zone as McGhee would like it to have been. An early flood of goals had faded to a trickle, and they failed to maintain the momentum initially generated.

Ironically, before the season had begun, Mark had been very complimentary about Wolves and how they had performed the previous season. The media at the time generally followed the line that, while Taylor had been a notoriously unsuccessful England manager, club management was very much his forte and it was predicted that he would do great things with Wanderers. He had been unlucky not to gain promotion into the Premiership.

Given this situation, with McGhee openly complimentary of the team's performance that season and of Taylor's management, how had it gone wrong for Wolves so quickly, leaving them in the mire that led to Taylor's removal and McGhee's arrival?

> 'There were a couple of things. They did have some injuries. One or two of the players that Taylor brought in didn't do as well initially as had been anticipated. Also, I think time had begun to catch up with some of the squad and the fact that they had failed to get promotion so narrowly the previous year meant that the crowd began getting impatient and in the end it just got to a lot of people. It left them unable to perform.'

Was morale especially low when Mark arrived in the middle of the season?

> 'It certainly seemed to be. There was a genuine fear of

relegation around the place. That was the first thing that we had to try and psychologically remove simply by trying to push people's confidence and to convince them that they were better than the position in the league suggested and that some people were now suggesting.'

What can you tell players in that unhappy, underconfident frame of mind?

'Right from the very beginning, I just talked very positively. I started talking about *promotion* through the play-offs. I never once mentioned relegation, I just kept talking in terms of the play-offs. I told them that they were better players than they had been showing and that I had *seen them* playing much better and expected that they would be better again. Everything was aimed at increasing everyone's confidence.'

How long does it take to do that? When the future's looking black, turning that corner back on to the road to recovery can surely be very difficult?

'In the long term, morale will only really increase with results.'

The season was practically over at the time we were having this conversation, and Mark was very realistic about Wolves' chances.

'I think it's too late *this* season. If we win a couple of games before the end, we can do a little better and possibly finish in the top half of the league.'

As it turned out, even that was not possible.

'Up until a game or two ago, we had averaged one and a half

> points per game since the arrival of me and my colleagues, and that's the sort of average that got everyone else in the play-offs. If we had averaged that all season, then, we *would* have been in the play-offs, so if we can achieve anything like that, then we can give people – not only the players who are going to be here, but the supporters in particular – great hope that, with the improvements we're going to make in terms of strengthening the squad, making them fitter, coaching them effectively in the forthcoming pre-season, we'll be able to make the difference between one and a half points per game and two, which would mean automatic promotion.'

Looking ahead to the future has always been a prominent part of Mark's approach. The long-termism he had spoken about at Leicester, he had taken with him across the Midlands.

> 'We can do things in the last four games of this season that will affect how we start the first game of next season. Players who achieve certain things and perhaps do particularly well in certain things we ask them to do over the next four games will take that through with them to kick-off next season, so we'll have a start on what we're trying to achieve already, rather than having to wait till the pre-season and seeing if we can do it then, so if we can do anything at this stage that's going to improve us, it'll hold us in good stead for next season.'

Mark always talks of 'we' and 'us'. Achievement for him is something gained collectively. This may surprise those who characterise him as a mercenary manager, moving from smaller to bigger clubs in pursuit of his undeniably strong personal ambitions. It seems that, whichever club he's with, for the time he is with it, he feels inseparable from its own destiny.

In two seasons, he had moved from Reading, through Leicester to Wolves. How big were these steps?

'There's a very big difference between Reading and here, and also a difference between here and Leicester, but much more noticeable in the case of Reading. It's not just cosmetic, either. It's not just in the size of the stadium. It's not just that we get twenty-six thousand people coming to watch us every week and they only get eight or nine at most. It's got everything to do with potential. Were Wolverhampton Wanderers to get promoted, we would think that we've got a relatively good chance of being the type of club that can survive in the Premier League. I'd say that it would have been unrealistic for a team like Reading, had they achieved the promotion which they nearly did last year, that they would survive a season up in the Premiership, unless the chairman made a total U-turn in his approach.'

A big lottery win, perhaps?

'He doesn't *need* to win the lottery! But if he suddenly started pouring some of his money into the club, that would be something new. The only way to survive in the Premier League is with top players and the only way to get top players is with top money. [Joe Kinnear would beg to differ here, I suspect.] And the only way you can get top money is either to earn it or have it within the club.'

For McGhee, getting to know individual players at a new club is something he doesn't feel is automatic for him. An admirer of Alex Ferguson, who he feels was able to size up particular players' needs quickly, he feels this does not come as readily to him:

'I think that knowing which buttons to push with which players is not something I am quite ready to do here at Wolves yet. On a Monday or a Tuesday with the players in private, you can get to know them a bit better having had time to reflect yourself. But to do it with real success, you have to know those people really well and I feel my colleagues and I haven't been here long enough for that yet.'

How big an impact have all the changes over the last couple of seasons been having on him? While some adapt well to change, generally speaking it always tends to be stressful. Has he felt that, or will he look back on it with a sense of happiness?

'In a sense, I will. But there has been a hell of a lot of stress and strain, as there was last season, moving to Leicester from Reading. There has been a great deal of turmoil and now we – that is to say, also Colin and Mike [Mark's coaching staff] and all our families – are ready for a sustained period of continuity in our lives. A period of stability is what this club needs as well. That's good, because it suits both the club and ourselves to think that way.

'Really, it's almost a case of me wanting to put these two years, or eighteen months, behind me and move ahead.'

To appreciate the impact of the moves of Mark McGhee to Wolves and Dave Bassett to Crystal Palace, it is necessary to look at the longer-term picture. In this book, it is only possible to look at what had happened when the end of the season arrived, but I suspect that to see the real consequences, a gap of a few seasons would be needed.

As it was, for Mark McGhee, the move had looked better three-quarters of the way through the season than at the very end. With the play-offs held up as possible, and all talk of relegation banished, Wolves had been averaging a point and a half per match in the aftermath of the managerial switch. Alas, this was not to last, and the club's performance petered out towards the end of the season, leaving Mark with clear plans for the future. No doubt changes would be made. Wolves finished twentieth in the table, only three points ahead of Millwall, who, at twenty-second, were relegated. It had ultimately been a close call. Nevertheless, Wolves fans had some cause for optimism. Before McGhee's arrival, relegation had seemed automatic, and Mark had saved the club from that, something he had been unable to do the previous season at Leicester.

In an ironic echo of that season, when Reading, the club he had left, had finished up in the play-offs (though they never managed to get promoted), so Leicester, the club he had left for Wolves, finished up in the play-offs this time. Mind you, given how strong they had been looking while he had been their manager, this is not too surprising. McGhee's successor, Martin O'Neill, although initially unpopular with the fans, following a string of indifferent results, had built on the work Mark had done with the team earlier to bring them to this point. They beat Bassett's Palace in the play-off finals, seeing Leicester through to the Premiership. All in all, fans of both Leicester and Wolves could be grateful for McGhee's contribution that season.

Graham Taylor, incidentally, as previous manager of Wolves, had gone to Watford, a club looking every bit as doomed at Wolves. Despite a valiant effort and some encouraging results late on in the season, for which coach Luther Blissett could also take a lot of credit, the club finished second from the bottom of the table, and went down.

Dave Bassett's efforts at Crystal Palace led to a more dramatic turn-around in fortune for the club. Struggling near the foot of the division when he arrived, Palace finished third, only four points behind second-place Derby County, who had thus obtained automatic promotion to the Premiership. For Palace to have secured automatic promotion would have been even more dramatic, but at least they were assured a place in the play-offs.

Intriguingly, the club that Bassett had left for Palace, also had something of a dramatic reversal of fortune. New manager Howard Kendall took them to ninth place in the table, making a change to the club's style of play as he did so, encouraging more of a passing game.

It seems that, in many cases, *any* change in manager is good for a club that has been doing badly (even, probably, in Watford's case, despite not being enough to save them). This is not to take anything away from the achievements of the managers discussed, but it does appear that the prospect of turning over a new leaf with a different manager, inevitable changes in coaching style, and the general feeling that a positive move has been made to halt the decline, can be enough to spur the players on to new heights. That this effect may wear off after a while, as do many other innovative moves, is something the manager must bear in mind. A change may be as good as a rest, but its beneficial effects are not going to last for ever. He'll have to have other tricks up his sleeve to keep the momentum going.

As I said, I've little doubt that, in the longer term, the moves of both managers to new clubs in the middle of this season are ones they will look back on without regret, but it will take longer for the full effects of their new regimes to make their impact on the clubs concerned.

Even so, Dave Bassett, in particular, had plenty to smile about – right up until the final match of the domestic season, anyway, when Palace weren't quite good enough to beat Leicester in those play-offs. Nevertheless, set against the club's position before his arrival, his contribution was clearly something to be proud of.

Naturally, he was asked what particular brand of witchcraft a man who had once dressed up as Mystic Meg for a national tabloid had used to achieve the dramatic improvement in Palace's results.

'I wish I could say I had some secret,' he replied. 'If I did, it would be worth millions.'

It would indeed. That much, at least, is certain.

11: The Lucky Jockstrap

'Oh won't you be my little good luck charm
Uh-huh-huh, you sweet delight
I want a good luck charm hangin' offa my arm
To have and to hold tonight.'

Elvis Presley

Football is famous for its superstitions – quirky, irrational beliefs that defy reason, common sense or, occasionally, even hygiene. Endless droll articles in the likes of *When Saturday Comes* expose fans' beliefs that eating cheese and onion crisps while sticking a finger up your nose will drive your team to victory, or listening to your favourite record played at the wrong speed before setting off to the match will somehow cause your keeper to keep a clean sheet. In *Fever Pitch*, Nick Hornby recounts how buying sugar mice, biting their heads off and throwing them under the wheels of passing traffic was thought to enhance a side's performance. It speaks volumes for the collective lunacy of being a football fan that we can read this and find it slightly amusing but, in the end, not at all unusual – rather than the behaviour of someone in a fairly advanced stage of schizophrenia.

Players are no better. Asking about superstitions has always been part and parcel of the 'Real Me' questionnaires found in such comics as *Shoot!*, *Match* and the *Sun*. And fascinating stuff it is, too. We can learn that a player always puts on a particular sock, takes it straight off and puts it back on again, convinced that this ritual will have some impact on his performance. We find that some players will only put their shirts on as they are just about to step out of the tunnel and on to the pitch, as if this will have a decisive effect on the result that afternoon. We hear of players refusing to wash their jockstraps or change their underpants if they associate these garments with a winning streak.

Needless to say, such ridiculous behaviour can make a manager's job more difficult.

The minute players start believing that what happens to them is significantly affected by luck (and with millions playing the lottery every week, are they really that unusual in such a belief?) is the minute they begin to question the extent to which defeat or victory rests on their performance. It is also the minute that they feel that the advice that a manager is giving them may be secondary to the whims of Lady Luck who, as everyone knows, is a fickle mistress.

The belief that players' destiny lies under their control, or if a less empowering manager is in charge, at least under *his* control, is crucial for a team's self-esteem. Psychologists call it having an *internal* Locus of Control. The idea that it may all be down to fluke is unsettling and demotivating. Faith in outside forces, too mysterious to be understood by anyone other than perhaps Mystic Meg, represents an *external* Locus of Control. If you really believe that what happens to you is somehow down to the whims of the gods, sitting up there and playing dice to decide your fate, the manager's influence is likely to be pretty negligible.

So how do managers view superstitions? Are they just a bit of harmless fun, or can a player's belief in luck seriously get in the way of getting the best performance out of him? After all, look at the players we read about who become very heavy gamblers. This 'mug punter' attitude can't help them take responsibility for their own actions, their own lives. And what of managers themselves? Do they have their own superstitions keeping them awake? Lucky rabbits' feet? Magic socks? Surely not . . .

'Yes, a lot of players do have superstitions,' agreed Dave Bassett.

'I don't get particularly involved with them. I'm not particularly superstitious myself.

'We've all gone through situations where perhaps if you've worn a tie and you're on a run, you suddenly think to yourself: "Well, I've worn this tie for the last four games. It must be a lucky tie." But then you realise you're losing and it's bugger all to do with the tie! Though I'm not that superstitious, I know that certain players like to sit in certain spots in the dressing room, they wouldn't want to wear a certain number, they like to wear their shorts in a special way or the shirt tucked out or the sock turned over or the boot tied in a certain manner.'

Are these things which players have been doing all their lives?

'No. I think it just triggers off sometimes. It just happens. I don't think it's something that they've done since they've been six years old. Perhaps a player has gone out laughing and has played an excellent game and it just triggers there and then.'

And does a manager ever need to stamp out a player's superstitious behaviour?

'I wouldn't get involved at all unless I thought the superstition was something stupid that was affecting the player. Perhaps a player gets used to eating a certain meal or going to bed at a certain time and he can get wrapped up in that. It's easy to do that. Sometimes it can become a comfort zone. The strong player says: "Bollocks to that! It's down to *me*. When I go out there, it's all down to how I perform on the day. Fuck the

> weather, fuck the stars, the sun, the clouds and everything else – I'm me and I'm the one who affects what goes on." But you need to be a strong person to think that, someone who's quite relaxed and at ease with themselves. Not all players are like that. Sometimes, if you force a player to change, he's going to feel disturbed and you'll end up getting a worse performance out of them. So you don't always know what's best.'

Knowing how seriously a superstition is affecting a player is clearly a bit of an art, though Joe Kinnear was quick to note that such beliefs among players are not necessarily all bad:

> 'I think superstition is a big part of the game. If you were to analyse any club – or any player – you'd find that, for example, certain players for some reason want to come last out of the tunnel. Or certain players want to be fourth. It's all psychological. It affects them mentally. Vinnie Jones is someone who at times will keep his shirt off as he's waiting in the tunnel before a match, and just as he comes out of the tunnel, he pulls it over his head. There are numerous examples. And if it works – why not? If it works for that player and gives him a little lift then there's no harm in it and no point in antagonising the player. I mean, you may make fun of it and the player can laugh it off at times, but if someone wants to go out last and that makes them happy, then I say you should let them.'

Mark McGhee agreed about the potential beneficial effects of having certain lucky rituals, but at the same time has seen some become a menace to a player's performance:

> 'I think superstitions can be a good thing in one sense. They can help the players to focus on what's important. They keep players tuned in to the fact that they've got a game coming up

or whatever. On the other hand, they can get in the way. I had a case when I first came to Leicester, a player who I'm sure won't mind me talking about it called David Lowe. He was a player who traditionally, as part of his routine, an hour before the game would go and lie in a hot bath and stretch his legs out for about twenty minutes. I had no idea for how long he had been doing this, but, as far as I'm concerned, that's totally the wrong thing to do! It tires your legs out.

'So one day I said to him: "Look, you're not doing that any more. I'm not allowing you to do that" and he said: "Wait a minute – I've done this for twelve years"! I replied: "Well, if you hadn't done that, maybe you'd be a better player, maybe you'd be playing for England." He still seemed unsure, so I said to him: "Just don't do it for this match and then next week, if you feel that not doing it affected you negatively, then you can do it again."

'And he's never done it since. He had got into a rut and had got himself to believe that he had to do it in order to be able to play. I think it's the same with all those kinds of superstitions. You just have to say: "You're not doing it!" If it's a case of a player feeling he can't play unless he's wearing something – hide it! If you do that, these things cease to be a problem.'

Can players play on the superstitions of others to unsettle them during the game?

'I don't think any of us are that clever. You would have to know a player inside out to be able to do that. It would be nice if you could!' Mark chuckled at the idea. 'I don't think it goes on much in real life.'

Players having individual superstitions is all very well, but what if some irrational beliefs are shared by more than one person? In fact, what if they affect a whole club?

McGhee's former team-mate, Tommy Burns, is glad it's not something he has to deal with.

'I think you find a lot of superstitions like that if you ask other people at other clubs, but not at Celtic Football Club, not to any extent that I'm aware of. Individual players may have superstitions, but I certainly don't, and I won't let them get in the way. You want people concentrating on a game of football, not whether their shirt should be out or which peg they've hung their tie on. But superstitions affecting everyone at a club is not a problem at Celtic.'

Not all managers are in this fortunate position. There is a famous story about Ron Saunders, former manager of Birmingham City, concerning a superstition that everybody in the club knew about and which was affecting the way his players performed. It seems that the club's stadium was the victim of an ancient gypsy curse. I know it sounds laughable enough to be something out of a short-lived comic strip somewhere in the middle of a very old issue of *Roy of the Rovers*, but it was evidently something that people at the club really considered a serious problem. Ron tried to deal with it by making the players wear boots whose soles had been dyed red and even went to the extent of performing an exorcism in the goal-mouth. Do do that voodoo that you do so well!

It's easy to laugh at such notions. So let's do it. Nevertheless, beliefs not as extreme as these, but just as damaging, can disrupt a team's performance. Most clubs have their 'bogey sides', teams to which they always seem to lose in defiance of all reason. Sometimes the club concerned is much smaller, and by rights shouldn't win at all, let alone on a regular basis. In other cases, it's simply the fact that a history exists of two sides playing and one always winning while the other always loses. Sometimes this can go on for years, as in the case of Hearts and Hibs in Edinburgh, the former permanent victors, the latter eternal losers, regardless of how either side performed against other clubs for the rest of the season.

'Yes, it can happen for particular clubs and it can happen for particular managers,' acknowledged Dave Bassett. 'There are certain teams you always seem to beat and there are certain teams you always lose against.'

The trick is to nip these things in the bud, prevent them ever starting in the first place. For Dave personally, it was important not to acquire his old side, Sheffield United, as a bogey side, following his mid-season move to Crystal Palace. By spooky coincidence, of the sort that would definitely merit investigation by agents Mulder and Scully of *The X-Files* (and which seems to occur with peculiar regularity in football – it's enough to turn anyone to superstition!), 'Harry' Bassett's former club were the first opponents he faced upon taking up the managerial reins at Palace. Eerie, or what?

> 'It was very uncanny and it was strange. But it affected me more in an emotional type of way. There's that feeling that it's your old club and you don't really need that, but it's not really a superstitious thing, more to do with emotion. It drains you. I was eight years at Sheffield United, and if you've been at a club that long, you get to know quite a few people there. It gets the imagination going, and you can become paranoid because you know that you left there and they desperately want to beat you. You begin to believe that there are demons there which you have to get rid of that afternoon.
>
> 'It happens to managers and, of course, to players too when they encounter a club they've been at before. My second game at Palace was against Watford, another club I had managed in the past!'

Just how much coincidence can a guy take?

> 'Having said that, when I was manager at Sheffield United, we played Watford . . . how many times? Let me think . . . seven times, so this was my eighth time facing my former club. That means there's less of an impact. But with Sheffield

> United, it was my first time facing them, my first game in charge of a new side, so it was very emotional.'

The Crystal Palace vs. Sheffield United match finished one each, so at least there isn't much danger of them becoming a bogey side for Dave in the future.

Of course, it's easy not to be superstitious when things are going well. When everything is great, then feeling that life is under your control, that you're responsible – or partly responsible – for things being as good as they are doesn't take too much effort. When things begin to go wrong, however, taking responsibility for *that*, admitting that the mistakes and the disappointments have been your doing too, is very much harder. That's why, looking back on Joe Kinnear's words from the beginning of the season, I wondered whether he still felt the same way after his slightly disappointing year.

> 'I don't believe in luck. I'm very dogmatic about it. I kick it into touch. I don't like players saying "We were unlucky" or "We didn't get the breaks" and, in fact, it's rare that you find our players using expressions like that, even to the press. All that business about hitting the post three times and this, that and the other is not something I like. I never try to look for ways out. If we've got beaten, then there's a reason why we've got beaten, and I look at that very carefully – unlike certain other managers!'

Who can he mean?

Where Joe does tend to apportion blame, it is not the whims of Lady Luck that concern him, but the errors of match officials – of which more anon – but it's tough to take a 'luck's got nothing to do with it' attitude when your club is languishing towards the bottom of the Premiership, as Wimbledon were for most of the later part of the season.

It is interesting that the managers interviewed talked about superstitions starting when things are going particularly well, but I think they are probably more likely to start when things are going badly. It is then that you don't want to blame yourself and so you evoke luck as an escape from having to do that.

This appears to affect even those at the very top. Surely a wily old Glaswegian like Alex Ferguson would have no time for superstitious mumbo-jumbo? A game late on in the season suggested that he just might, when Manchester United travelled to the Dell to face Southampton, full of confidence that the Premiership was theirs. Former favourites Newcastle had had a series of frustrating losses, and now even the Geordies were beginning to suspect that the Championship trophy might again be going to Old Trafford.

Southampton should, by all accounts, have been fairly straightforward. Struggling badly at the opposite end of the table, only their reputation as a 'bogey team' for several more successful sides stood in their favour (shrewd observers thought that Man United had been lucky to beat them at their previous encounter). By half-time, Southampton were 3–0 up!

It was at this point that Alex Ferguson was to demonstrate that he was no stranger to superstition himself and, no doubt trying to placate Lady Luck, who would have grown very irritable at Man United's cockiness, got his side to change shirts at half-time from grey to blue. The grey shirt had been steadily acquiring a reputation for being associated with doom and gloom. The Reds (blues/ blacks/greys, et cetera) had already lost to Arsenal and struggling Coventry in these kits. What went on in the dressing room, I've no idea. Whether Ferguson really believed that a change of shirt would bring about a change of luck, or whether he felt that as long as the players believed this was the case, the team might be in with a chance, he gave it a go. If Locus of Control had rapidly externalised, and everything was being blamed on the shirts, it was time to internalise it again and remind the players that it was all down to them – though, just to be on the safe side, the shirts would go.

Well, they scored one goal. I suppose 3–1 is a tiny bit better than 3–0. It just goes to show, though, that when suddenly things are beginning to go wrong, it takes a strong will not to start bringing luck into the equation.

The grey shirt story captured everyone's imagination. There were even some who suggested that grey was a more difficult colour for the eye to pick out, though the evidence was not wholly convincing (in fact, it wasn't remotely convincing), and the general consensus seemed to be that Alex was talking superstitious twaddle to cover up his embarrassment over the result. There were no enquiries from the Magic Circle about how such shirts could be incorporated into tricks in which people have to vanish, or from the army about any uses such garments might have as camouflage gear. The club instantly announced, however, that the shirt would never be worn by any player again, as it was being scrapped in favour of a brand-new design which would shortly become available.

This could be an example of swift reaction to a major scare. (Those involved in selling things to football supporters are known for their rapid response to a crisis – when fears escalated over the safety of British beef, I noticed that the burger vans outside Highbury for the match against Newcastle had hastily improvised hand-written reassurances that their products were really lamb burgers, and thus nothing to worry about at all.) It could, alternatively, be an example of wily marketing folk cashing in on humiliating publicity and turning it to a club's advantage. I'll let the reader decide.

I felt it best, nevertheless, to check with Terry Venables, whether the story would cause widespread panic in the England camp. England, after all, also possessed a grey kit which they sometimes wore. What did he make of claims that grey shirts at night might be Croatia's delight?

'Hmmmmmm. Interesting point. I'll have to bear it in mind,' was all he had to say on the matter.

When England came to play their next match, however, they were wearing their grey shirts for all to see (or perhaps not see?), so the seriousness of the threat might not be so great after all, given a couple of seconds' consideration. No one was turned invisible, though Robbie Fowler might have wished that he had been, given a performance that was singled out, somewhat unfairly, by the tabloids that had demanded his inclusion in the side, largely over one missed opportunity. The fans might have wanted more excitement than the goalless draw that they got, but compared to Man U's demolition by Southampton, it was a much more even-handed contest. It seemed that grey would stay. Superstition may be rife in the game, but there are limits.

Having said that, the following England match, which finished in a 3–0 defeat of Hungary, was played with white shirts.

'See? It must have been the shirts!' I told Terry Venables that evening.

'Had to be! That's the explanation!' he grinned.

The team then went off on their tour of the Far East, where they beat China 3–0 (white shirts) and struggled to beat a select Hong Kong eleven, full of players who were, not to put too fine a point on it, getting on a bit in years, 1–0 (grey shirts). Spooky, or what?

At Newcastle, meanwhile, beaten by Liverpool in a match many neutral supporters felt was one of the best in years, and defeated by Blackburn thanks to two last-minute goals, Kevin Keegan commented that his assistant Terry McDermott believed the team was jinxed. Keegan himself refused to go along with it.

However, when things are crumbling around you, particularly when they were once going so well, even the most rational, cynical pragmatist can begin to look out for black cats and cracks in the pavement.

I speak from personal experience here. As I was researching this book, I found myself actually become part of the mythology surrounding Dulwich Hamlet's pattern of results, watching a superstition grow, from a bit of a laugh, through a bit of a laugh but

– who knows? – there may be something there, to the point where I had just about begun to believe it myself.

I had been offered the opportunity to accompany the team on some of its away matches to see how manager Frank Murphy maintained team spirit, timed his team talks and so on. Naturally, away matches are harder to win, so it wasn't too great a surprise that they lost a few of the matches I watched. It was then pointed out that, even when I went to home matches, my presence was associated with the side losing. You can laugh this off for a while, and cite a couple of matches where the side had drawn, or even won ('Ah, but you left that one early . . .'), but once it's established that you may be a jinx, it's hard to shake off. Of course, everyone treated it as a joke at first, but the more it happened, the more I wondered whether anyone might be taking it seriously.

My initial plan was to turn up at a match where the side achieved an emphatic victory, thereby quashing any talk of a jinx once and for all. Unfortunately, the more I tried this, the less it happened, so just to be on the safe side, I stayed away for most of the second half of the season. I'd like to say that Dulwich Hamlet won the league as a result, but they didn't, which shows what superstitious rubbish the whole thing was. No one *really* believes in jinxes, and yet . . .

I needed to come back down to earth with a healthy bit of Caledonian pragmatism from Mark McGhee. I talked to him about Spurs under Ardiles and their string of appalling results. Players had seemed to lose all self-belief and could easily have felt jinxed. Mark was having none of it.

'I'm not sure whether it was down to superstition when you look at Ossie Ardiles' record at Spurs, because we had him at Newcastle when I was a player there and he wasn't a lot different there, to be honest!' he pointed out.

So there you have it. Let's keep a sense of proportion here. After all, who needs jinxes, when you've got Ossie Ardiles?

12: The Villains No Longer Wear Black

'It takes some believing for a referee to mix up two players as different in appearance as we are. I'm five foot eight inches and white. He's six foot four inches and black.'

Plymouth player Tony Spearing, 1992

These days, the villains tend to wear green.

I refer, of course, to referees, whose attempts to impose structure and discipline on a game may be very much at odds with those of the manager. The manager can suggest to players that they may like to do this or that. He can be gentle in that suggestion, or he can be as forceful as he likes. If he wants to throw a few teacups around and shout a bit, he can. But, in the end, he can only suggest and hope that a player takes the suggestion seriously. A referee, on the other hand, can *order* players to do things and send them off if they disagree. Referees have the rulebook and, by implication, the collective might of the Football Association behind them. This amounts to ninety minutes of pure power, while the manager can only sit and squirm on the sidelines – and if he's tempted to do otherwise, the ref can throw the book at him, too.

This wouldn't matter so much if referees could be relied upon, if they showed consistency in their decision-making, if you knew where you stood with them. Lately, however, the man in the middle, never a popular figure at the best of times, has been making more and more strange decisions, evoking in his defence FIFA's constant changes to the rulebook and the fact that a ref is increasingly forced to apply the letter, rather than the spirit, of the law, whether he likes it or not. They say a good ref is one whom nobody notices as the game is played. Well, if any such refs exist, they can bask in happy anonymity. The very fact you may know a ref's name or what he looks like must mean that he can't be any good.

The idea that refs should be made professional has been knocking around for some time. As things stand, they are volunteers who do other jobs to make a living and, like secret transvestites, don alternative clothing for evenings and weekends to assume their other role. For this they are paid a fraction of the manager's salary, which shrinks even further when compared with what some players in the Premiership earn. So why do they do it? Pride? Megalomania? Wanting to participate in a game they were never able to play themselves at a high level (when did anyone hear of a footballer going on to become a ref?), or just the love of performing in front of a huge crowd? None of these motives sounds very honourable and some of them sound distinctly perverse, so it's no surprise that no one loves a referee when he's forty (or any other age). Fans, players and, crucially, managers will all have bad memories of astonishing refereeing decisions somewhere along the line. What can they do about them? Do they have any sympathy for refs? Can adverse referee decisions be turned to a team's advantage by adopting a 'Well, the ref seems to have got it in for us, but we'll show *him*' mentality during the half-time team talk?

Perhaps the most memorable ridiculous refereeing decision of the season (though not necessarily the worst – there were so many) concerned Walter Smith's Rangers. Fired up for Hogmanay, the blue half of Glasgow made mincemeat of Edinburgh's Hibs. The 7–0 thrashing, featuring a hat trick by Gordon Durie, was everything Rangers fans could have wanted and more, but the match will always be remembered by those who saw it, or who caught the subsequent clips on the box, for the painfully humourless behaviour of referee Dougie Smith (no relation) and his exchange with Paul Gascoigne.

Gazza, in keeping with the general on-pitch wackiness which has always been part of his style, found that the referee had dropped his yellow card. Picking it up to give it back to him, Gascoigne improvised a little routine that could have earned him a place on *Whose Line Is It Anyway?* which involved pretending to book himself with the card in question and then, as an added flourish, pretending to book the ref, just before returning his lost property. It came as something of a surprise to everybody watching, when the ref promptly booked the jovial player with the very object he had just been handed back. What a card, as the headlines might have put it (and almost certainly did).

Watching the player's expression at this point was a must for those who are into reading body language. After all, Gazza is likely to have painful memories of yellow cards generally (who can forget Italia '90, where one such offending item had seen to it that, had England beaten West Germany, Paul would not have been allowed to play in the final – cue all those tears?) and incidents like this can't do much for anyone's confidence. As he turned round, however, the player was clearly smiling – the sheer ridiculousness of the booking preventing even the person booked from taking it entirely seriously. He went on to score a superb goal.

This was just the most obvious symptom of a much deeper disease. There were to be more bookings for Gazza, some justified, others controversial. Another actually led to the resignation of the referee concerned, who stated that pressure to follow the rules to the letter had made his job an impossible one. The Scottish press were full of stories about the decline in the quality of refereeing over the years, and things were no better south of the border. Was this really an accurate observation, or had the increasing amount of scrutiny provided by the fact that more and more matches are now televised simply highlighted a problem that was as old as the hills? And what did managers make of these decisions and indeed of today's breed of ref, those complete and utter bastions of Association-appointed integrity?

I asked Walter Smith, Gazza's gaffer at Rangers, what he made of it:

> 'I think that particular decision was a one-off. You're not likely to get too many of those! It has been shown very widely on television all over Britain and I think that even most of the referees watching say they wouldn't have reacted in that manner to that situation. Referees themselves just now are being placed in a terrible position. They're being more or less told exactly how to referee matches and precisely what they must do to a particular player in a particular situation. It's not being left to their discretion at all.
>
> 'I think that taking away that discretion has taken away a lot of the rapport referees once had with players. I think players would always respect that a referee makes his decision fairly and would in fact talk to the referee quite a lot during the game. Nowadays that doesn't happen nearly as much, which not only means that the players tend to respect the decisions less, but it also leaves the referee feeling very isolated.'

Some managers have a reputation for being very outspoken about what they deem to be unfair refereeing decisions after the match, regardless of whether or not this might get them in hot water with the authorities. This may seem like a way of venting spleen in the heightened emotional atmosphere that exists in the immediate wake of a loss. But can it serve a deeper purpose? By criticising a referee, a manager might not only be protecting the self-esteem of his own players but also encouraging team mentality: 'It's us against that ref and we won't let the bastard break our spirits.'

Indeed, Joe Kinnear is one manager who has acquired something of a reputation for this. His disagreements with referees have been well documented elsewhere, including Wimbledon's idea of putting together a video to demonstrate just how victimised the club had been. Walter Smith gave his view:

> 'If you want to use it that way, you can, but you can end up in total isolation by encouraging that type of mentality. In the end, every one of us has to live by the referee's decision. Sometimes, though, to be fair to Joe, he's been on the receiving end of some very bad decisions indeed. I'm not sure whether it is an intentional thing to build that kind of mentality. I would rather look at it as a manager feeling totally aggrieved that he had been dealt with unfairly, that he hadn't had a fair crack of the whip in the way the decisions went. One thing I strongly feel all of us have to do to make players feel better is constantly to point out that bad refereeing decisions are not always directed towards the same players or towards the same team. It can be a dangerous thing if you start saying that bad decisions are continually being levelled at your team and your players to a greater extent than anybody else's. It's good for players to learn that there will be bad decisions made against them, but that they can stand up and get on with it and not let it affect them. If you blame the referee too much, it can sometimes take the onus off the players, and they have to learn to deal with it.'

Another Scot, Mark McGhee, broadly agrees:

> 'It can certainly affect players if a decision goes against them that they feel hard done by, but I think it's not something you can dwell on. Referees are human beings and are likely to make mistakes, but these generally balance themselves out over the season. We've had bad decisions against us here – *very* bad decisions – but, equally, there have been decisions when we have turned to look at one

another and said: "Well, we were a little bit fortunate there!" It does even itself out.'

This season saw quite a change in the behaviour of Eric Cantona, previously a player who had a lot of trouble with referees. The transformation from seething cauldron of uncontrolled Gallic urges to model professional who no doubt helps ageing fans across the road (*Red Devil Turns Angel!*, or something equally obvious, as one of the tabloids almost certainly put it) had certainly had a lot to do with manager Alex Ferguson's coaching. Knowing that Mark had been a great admirer of Alex during the former's playing days, when Ferguson had been his manager at Aberdeen, I asked him what could be done to make players more 'referee-friendly'.

'Someone at Wolverhampton who has been a little bit guilty this season of the same kinds of things as Cantona last season has been Steve Bull. His is a very aggressive style. Yet Steve Bull has been riding for about ten games with the spectre of one more booking being needed to cause him suspension, and has managed to come through without getting booked.'

Could this be down to what you told him upon arriving at Wolves?

'Well, the point now is educating players as to their responsibilities, their importance to the team and just how important it is that we don't lose players because they are suspended. You will always lose players because they are injured, you have to live with that, but you shouldn't lose players for silly reasons. Players are now learning to be more responsible, knowing how the team will suffer if they are prevented from playing through suspension. I mean, there are certain bookings that you'll never cut out, but I think you see less and less nowadays – certainly here at Molineux you do. You don't see so many of the silly bookings for time-wasting or for kicking the ball away or for encroaching and that sort of thing any more. Having said that, we had a player booked at Sheffield United last week. It was nil–nil, with ten minutes gone, and one of our players had a throw-in with no one to throw it to, about twenty yards from our by-line. The referee booked him for not taking it quickly enough! That, for me, is scandalous. That's a defender who could easily end up tripping somebody later, just a wee innocuous trip, get a second booking and have to go off. So there *are* some very poor decisions being made sometimes in the game today.'

Is there a temptation to be very outspoken about it when you feel that a decision has gone against you?

'I think I've "lost the place" at times with referees and I've often regretted it. Not because there have been repercussions, but simply because, when you go away, in the light of day and in quietness, you get to realise that referees are human. In addition to that, the decisions which you jump up and down and remonstrate about at the time, turn out to have been good decisions! I had this very thing myself – I wish I could remember the chap's name – when we had a linesman lining our game at Exeter a couple of years ago, when I was still with Reading. I absolutely slaughtered him, when I thought he made two decisions which took us from being four–one up at half-time to being four each within about ten minutes of the start of the second half. I thought he'd given two absolutely diabolical decisions, so I absolutely lambasted this linesman, who was right in front of us and, to be honest, given my language and all that, I just "lost the place".

'Now, the reality was that when I saw it on the TV, neither of the goals were offside, as I had thought at the time of the match, and even before I had seen it on the TV, I had realised that I had been totally out of order. I actually sent a letter to this official, apologising for my behaviour, because it had been totally uncalled for. I'd lost my temper not because he had made a couple of bad decisions, but because my players had allowed Exeter City to go from four–one to four each in the space of ten minutes. I was taking it out on the linesman, and it was totally unfair.

'As it was, he took the abuse and I know that he wrote back to me and appreciated my letter, but that was certainly one incident which taught me to take things a bit more easy.'

Dave Bassett hasn't always seen eye to eye with referees either, though he sees dangers in criticising them spiritedly. Contrary to what some may believe, it doesn't necessarily endear you to your players:

'Sometimes the team might think that the manager having a go at the referee is counterproductive, and the referee might turn against *them*. It can work that way, with the players looking at an instance of the manager criticising the ref and wishing that he wouldn't. Having said that, in America, you can have rows between referees and baseball players, and there's an openness there. Unfortunately, football is slightly different in that respect. We have to respect the rules, but that doesn't always mean to say that the rules are right. A lot of rules are archaic in football . . .'

Jim Smith is another who sympathises with the plight of the modern referee. A policeman's lot is not a happy one? Peanuts compared to those who dispense the law on the field, it would appear.

'I feel a bit sorry for them, in all honesty. They have got so many pressures on them now and so many decisions have been taken out of their hands. Common sense doesn't come

> into it now and consequently we're now all used to controversial decisions.
>
> 'The only thing we can do as managers, and it's very difficult, is to make sure that your players respond in a positive way to those decisions, rather than getting more frustrated and more angry and losing the place.'

Exactly the same expression was used by Mark McGhee. 'Losing the place' is clearly a well-established football term, and has nothing to do with someone nicking your parking spot. Jim went on:

> 'The last thing you want is players being booked or sent off for actions they can actually control, so that's all a football manager can do, really. The fact that you get certain managers being very outspoken about refereeing decisions probably isn't some kind of psychological ploy to get the team behind them – it might be occasionally, but those cases would be few and far between. The reason managers can explode over the decisions made by refs is that frequently those decisions will have a bigger impact on the career of the manager than they will on that of the player. That is absolutely the fact.'

So there we are. Perhaps reading deep psychological motives into public criticism of referees is barking up the wrong tree. Managers are human, just as players and supporters are human. Referees represent the biggest threat to a manager's power in the game – apart from chairmen and directors. Chairmen and directors at least employ you. Referees and other officials just turn up, get paid a pittance compared to everyone else involved in the game, and yet for the duration of the match wield supreme power. It's not nice. Even Matthew Le Tissier was sent off this season. Perhaps with the refereeing guidelines that exist now, even the saintly Gary Lineker might have fallen foul of the ref's yellow – even (whisper it!) red – card.

We already know Dave Bassett's views, expressed in a separate chapter, that football is turning into a game for pansies, in that draconian officials are stifling the competitive spirit intrinsic to the sport. It seems they're not doing much for the blood pressure of those forced to sit and watch on the sidelines, either.

One unforgettable image of Graham Taylor from the programme made about him occurred as the sun was already setting on his career, as England's defeat by Holland put paid to any hopes of qualification for the World Cup USA in 1994. He was seen, puce in the face, steam practically flying from his ears, shouting at the linesman.

'He's cost me my job. That man's cost me my job . . .' he kept repeating.

Well, the finger of blame can't be pointed exclusively at that one individual, but you can see how Taylor felt. And even if the referee or any other official isn't to blame, he makes a convenient scapegoat to cover up any managerial inadequacies which may also have contributed.

This is where the fans come into their own. At least they can be relied upon to give the referee hell, a bittersweet pleasure not available to players, managers or, as Sam Hammam knows, club owners. In that respect, the fans have more power than they probably realise, and they will continue to exercise that power, until, as I witnessed at this year's Arsenal–Newcastle clash at Highbury, they get slung out for using foul and abusive language.

Never has the twelfth man had a more important role to play.

13: Of Carrots, Sticks and Turnips

Robbie Elliot: *We got excited one night and thought it would be funny to spray Steve Howey with a fire extinguisher. Next thing we knew, Clarkey had a hold of it and he thought he was a Ghostbuster, running up and down the corridors.*

Steve Watson: *The hotel manager didn't think it was funny and we were fined and had to buy another fire extinguisher. Childish schoolboy pranks!*

Talk of the Toon: *What did the manager have to say about that?*

Steve Watson: *Luckily, it was only Ossie. It would never happen now.*

Interview in the fanzine *Talk of the Toon*

There are times when managing a football team and teaching in a primary school don't seem to be quite as far apart as they should. Occasional outbursts by a manager after a noticeably poor performance sometimes echo the exasperation of a schoolteacher who has just had to endure an hour and a half of psychological torture at the hands of a class of little monsters. Indeed, the Honey Monster, who, in an old Sugar Puffs commercial, made a schoolmistress's hair stand on end, turned up on our television screens more recently playing for Newcastle United, under the watchful eye of Kevin Keegan. This advert has had a couple of interesting consequences. Firstly, it has apparently led to a sharp drop in the sales of a certain breakfast cereal in the Sunderland area, and secondly, it has served to remind us all that footballers are frequently big kids at heart, not long out of short trousers and pestering exhortations if not to tell 'em about the honey, Mummy, then at least something similarly hedonistic.

What can managers do? Half of their team may be adults, but the other half are still just boys, in spirit and sometimes even in age. Dennis Wise may look as though he's still at school, but there are many more players who act as though they are. After all, with managers telling them what to do and what not to do, the average away match is not a million miles from a coach trip to the seaside.

How does a manager keep discipline? Being tolerant is all very well, but what if that doesn't work and he has to go further? How does he handle it? After all, no one wants a reputation as a bit of a wimp when it comes to reading the riot act. Ossie Ardiles' 'live and let live' attitude may have endeared him to some players but, despite his legal background, laying down the law didn't seem to come naturally to him and might well have contributed to his rather woeful record as a manager (not to be confused with his other woeful record, the one with Chas and Dave, which changed for ever the public's perception of how to pronounce Totting-ham).

There is also the other extreme, of course, which came to everyone's attention following an incident at Grimsby Town in February of this season. Manager Brian Laws lost his temper with Italian star Ivano Bonetti and somehow – no one knows quite how – the player ended up in hospital, being operated on to repair a fractured cheekbone and free a trapped nerve. The official explanation concerned hurled crockery. Whatever really went on, the words of that song about the conversations with the flying plates were echoed when player and manager confirmed it was great to be in love again and the club got on with its successful FA Cup run, beating West Ham 3–0 the following day.

That one may have been sorted out, but there are several other tales doing the rounds of players and managers being involved in exchanges which got physical. One Premiership manager (whom I won't name, as libel actions can be expensive) is rumoured to have actually punched a player unconscious in one of his earlier management jobs, tendering his resignation immediately afterwards. This is some way from Ardiles' 'let the children have their fun' approach.

Jim Smith agrees that being able to balance reward and punishment effectively is more a part of a manager's job today than ever before:

> 'It is very important. I've always done it, in all honesty, but I think it's more important today in as much as society has changed a lot and you've got to know whether to treat players as people or as kids – they mainly *are* kids when they first come to your club, but they're not educated the same way as we were when we were at school. In those days, if the headmaster said something, we did it and if the teacher said something, we did that. Nowadays attitudes are totally different and players feel that they have got more to offer than just to listen to what you have got to say.
>
> 'More and more players who I come into contact with need the softly softly approach. They can't take the heavy hand. They go under. That's because they're not used to it. We had to fight for everything when we were younger, but they don't have to fight for too much nowadays. It's just a reflection of society and you have to come to terms with that, just as you have to come to terms with the bloody amounts of money that they earn! These are all things that take getting used to.'

The sensitivity of today's player is very apparent. Witness Chris Waddle's inability to take penalty kicks after a couple of humiliating misses, most obviously in the semi-finals of the 1990 World Cup, or Jason Lee's loss of confidence, blamed by Nottingham Forest manager Frank Clark on the continual digs he received on the comedy show *Fantasy Football League*, which led to such a drop in form that the player was put on the transfer list.

So has Smith's style changed over the years, as players' attitudes have changed?

> 'Yes. I think that as you get older, you change your style any road, but I haven't changed it all that dramatically because I've never really been the "sergeant major" type.'

The same system of reward and punishment can be used to get the best out of players on the pitch, he would argue:

> 'When there's been a bad result, you've got to look at the overall picture – where the team is in the league, what point it is in the season, how much pressure there is on and so on and then you decide what your best options are. You may go for the stick and hammer them for a week, work them doubly hard, or you may feel that they've been hammered too much and offer the carrot – take them away for a few days, or give them a couple of days off, or organise a golf day. You've got to try these things out and see how players respond at different times in the season.
>
> 'Prior to our crucial game against Palace, we took them away to Leeds for a couple of days, where we took them out to a restaurant for a meal, golfed 'em, trained 'em, sent them home to their families on Saturday, and then we played the match on Sunday. Needless to say, we won two–one.
>
> 'It's hard to get to know players as individuals to start with, but as a result of doing things like that, you eventually get to

know which ones you need to give a kick up the backside and which ones you need to put your arm round. You've got to get the balance right, and that's one of the hardest aspects of the manager's job, because what you'd really like to do is to treat everybody the same way, and be equal and fair. But you can't do that. Some players can take a rollocking but, as I've said, some tend to go under. I tend to relax players and take as much of the pressure off, just tell them calmly to keep doing the right thing, rather than use the rod.'

On-pitch discipline is one thing. Crimes and misdemeanours off the pitch are something else.

One thing vital to Joe Kinnear when it comes to disciplining a player is the element of confidentiality:

'I'm very much a hands-on manager, and if there's anything going on, I like to nip it in the bud on that particular day. If someone says something or does something they shouldn't, I like to address it immediately. I get them to go upstairs to my office and I say: "I don't want you to do that, I don't want you to say that ever again, I don't want to listen to this crap, this isn't going to happen any more, it's bollocks" or whatever. I have to make it clear that the behaviour of the player isn't doing me, the team or the club any good at all and that's it – it's finished. I don't want to be reading about it in the papers. That's how I work. If we're going to wash our dirty linen, we won't do it in public. We'll do it in my office or, occasionally, in the dressing room.

'I have never gone to the press and slated a player who wore a Wimbledon shirt. Players can have a bad day, as can we all.'

Dave Bassett has a reputation for being adept at being able to combine having a laugh with the lads on the one hand, with a firm sense of discipline on the other. Other managers with this skill also spring to mind (Keegan certainly seems well equipped to deal with the indiscretions of Honey Monsters and other players alike). Others still find it difficult to do both, leaving their players confused with their sudden mood swings from party animal to Old Testament prophet. Tommy Docherty's early days as manager of Chelsea were characterised by rapid swings, according to those who played under him, from sweetness and light one moment to blood and thunder the next.

How does Bassett do it?

> 'I treat every case individually. That's how you build up your respect and your loyalty. Successful man-management is all about how you deal with things. You don't always take the same approach. You look at the situation, try and find out as many facts about it as you possibly can, and then you have to decide whether you're going to take action. That can be by suspending a player, fining him, not fining him but making him do extra duties, whatever the situation demands.'

Has he ever been in a situation where he had to sell a player because of indiscretions committed?

'No.'

Does it ever happen?

> 'I think it's largely an invention of the press, though sometimes you may decide that a player has gone far enough and that he needs to go, because perhaps he's got himself into trouble in the city and there are people looking for him or people picking on him, so it's in the player's interest as much as the club's.'

Can it really be the case that a club like Liverpool would sell a player like Don Hutchison solely because of a couple of incidents involving drunken indecent exposure? (To the player's misfortune, videos and snaps of the incidents concerned all found their way to the *News of the World*.)

> 'I could believe that one. Liverpool might have decided that in that particular case, it was behaviour unbecoming for a player of that club. You never really know. Sometimes there could be a time when, because of a player's behaviour, you decide that to sell him is better for him and it's better for us. Those things can come. But if a player gets done for drink-driving or whatever, you don't decide to sell him there and then. It's outside the club. Obviously it is a problem and you have to deal with it, but I like to judge players on their football ability and prowess and what they're doing in the club.'

What about the way that Arsenal and the FA dealt with Paul Merson's admission of alcoholism and cocaine-snorting? Was that a progressive move?

> 'I just thought Merson opened his gob and dropped everybody else in the shit, really. He got paid for his admission and I think that he and Chris Armstrong [who tested positive for cannabis during a random FA drugs test] got away with murder, really. I mean, the FA didn't fine them. All right, they wouldn't let them play for a while, but they got no fine and the FA sent them away, paid for their rehabilitation, and I think it stinks, quite honestly. George Graham lost his job and they've admitted taking bloody drugs! Ben Johnson was banned for two years. I think this is another situation where there are double standards.'

I suppose the fact that the drugs were taken for recreational rather than performance-enhancing purposes might have influenced the FA?

'I am not saying they did it to improve their performance, but it's still drugs, isn't it? Either it's illegal or it's not. I mean, if you take a Lemsip because you've got a cold, it counts as an illegal drug. Neither of those players have thought about their clubs. They haven't taken a responsible attitude. Chris Armstrong had to miss games. If he hadn't, Crystal Palace might have stayed up, mightn't they? I thought it was just another whitewash and the FA failed to deal with the problem again – definitely double standards. Players look at that and they think: "Oh, that's good! If I fancy drugs, I'll go to the FA, tell them about it and they'll send me somewhere and dry me out, rehabilitate me, and it'll be all right. Nothing happens to me and I'm back playing again when I want to." '

How big a problem is the availability of drugs among young players?

'Oh, I'll bet you most players have sampled some drug at some stage, whether at a party or whatever. I'm not saying they're all drug addicts, but drugs are there to be had and I'm sure it's not just Merson and Armstrong. They're the ones who got caught though, aren't they?'

Harry's views are likely to have been shared by others in football and the FA must have picked up the murmurings, because February of this season saw a decision very different in spirit to that affecting Merson and Armstrong the previous one. Leyton Orient defender Roger Stanislaus was banned by the FA for a year and booted out of his club for taking a performance-enhancing drug. He tested positive for cocaine, which seemed to have been taken on match day, though the player claimed that he had taken it several days previously, at a funeral (I've heard of people wanting their friends at the wake to have a good time when they're gone, but this is taking things to new levels). This defence was not thought to be convincing (a story all too familiar where Orient defenders are concerned), as it seemed that the quantity the player had taken would have had to have been several times the lethal dose for it to have stayed in his system that long. Stanislaus would hardly have consumed a quantity of the stuff that even Keith Richards would balk at, and anyway, chairman Barry Hearn is unlikely to have been paying his players enough to afford that sort of amount.

There were some important differences between this case and those of Merson and Armstrong – not just, as cynics might point out, that Orient are a much smaller club than Arsenal or Crystal Palace. Armstrong had only tested positive for a soft drug, one unlikely to be of much value in performance enhancement (unless a languid, chilled-out performance was specifically required). Merson didn't test positive at all, and some feel that he only mentioned sampling cocaine because his real problems, alcoholism and an addiction to gambling, were not sufficiently interesting to the press on their own. Stanislaus, on the other hand, had tested positive for a hard drug which was potentially performance-enhancing and had then tried to wriggle out of it. The FA could justify coming down harder this time, but I suspect that the feeling that Merson, Armstrong and others had got off lightly in the past also played a part.

At Rangers, Walter Smith offered another perspective on drugs and football:

> 'A situation like the one involving Merson is very rare. One of the things I like to do as a manager is to treat everyone fairly and in a similar way. That type of situation doesn't really lend itself to this approach, so it is very difficult to say how I would handle it. I would have to look at that individual and try to decide what is best for him, and also what is best for the club. In those circumstances, I would seek advice from those who have encountered these problems before – not necessarily in

football, but in some other walks of life – to try and make sure that I was doing the right thing.

'But I must admit, the Paul Merson thing started me thinking. We have a drug rehabilitation group here called Calton Athletic, who are a football team. I got them to come in and talk to all our younger players, the apprentices and the first year professional players, just to discuss the issues and make the players aware that drugs are more readily available now to young kids than ever before. So that was an offshoot of the publicity around the Paul Merson case. As for what I'd do if I encountered it among my own players, though, I'd have to seek external advice, and I'm sure that George Graham and the English FA did, too.'

Calton Athletic (not to be confused with Charlton Athletic) have become well known for their work with young addicts and using football to build a sense of purpose and achievement. The group's story was dramatised in a television play with Robbie Coltrane and Lennie Henry, and members of the team even appeared in the kick-around which features at the beginning of the film *Trainspotting*, but that's about a Hibs supporter, so it may not be wise to mention it here.

But aside from a dependence on drugs, which is still if not unique then unusual, what about other off-field activities that might affect a player? After all, Paul Merson's main problems were drink and betting . . .

'You can never be sure what a player is doing off the field, no matter what anybody says. Your first indication is in training: a lack of enthusiasm; some of your livelier characters being unusually quiet or whatever. You hope that you can notice these things fairly quickly and if there's something that the club can do, then we try to do it. We speak to the player, find out what kind of problem it is and what we can do to help. A lot of the time it's not possible, we can't do anything. But you do get players with personal problems – all clubs do – and we try to lend a sympathetic ear here from the chairman and directors downwards. I like to feel that everybody at the club should provide an environment where the players can be at their best, and that includes helping them out with any personal problems they may have. We're all pulling in the same direction.'

Mark McGhee tries to take a similarly enlightened approach. But is a manager's approach to discipline inevitably influenced by the managers that have worked with him in the past, during his time as a player, or a coach?

'I think every manager should have a unique approach, in the sense that I don't think you can *copy* anybody's style. I believe your own style evolves. Here at Wolves, we are the types who don't dwell on the negative, but prefer to concentrate on the positive, thereby attempting to encourage people and to build them up, regardless of what we feel inside about what's actually happening. You can't berate people and slag them off without it having an effect on them. Some managers I know are very critical of different players, but others take a different approach. One of those is Fergie, who used to be my manager at Aberdeen. He was able to cope with individuals. Thus, within, say, a half-time team talk, he knew which players he could get away with slagging off, which ones he should praise and so on in order to get a better performance in the second half. He was able to do that in those fifteen minutes – or ten minutes, as it was then.

'I tend to find myself that I'm not as particular as that, especially having come to Wolves this season. I tend to sweep with a broader brush and try to be positive with them all.'

Certainly, the time Ferguson invested in helping Eric Cantona was well worth it. Following what is euphemistically called 'The Incident' in increasingly hushed tones by increasingly reverent journalists, the Manchester United manager focused on improving his player's behaviour, with remarkable results. Voted Player of the Year by journalists in the 1995–96 season, he had been a model of good behaviour since his return from suspension, the punishment for karate-kicking a spectator (who then got into all kinds of courtroom trouble himself) on his way off the pitch, following a red card.

That might have been a 'just off-pitch' incident, but to what extent does what happens to players away from the park affect their performance and what can managers do to discipline or help them?

Mark McGhee is in no doubt about how much of an effect circumstances off the pitch may have: 'They can affect a player totally. More often than not, if a player loses his form, it is exactly for that reason. Confidence and peace of mind are ninety per cent of a player. A player of the greatest ability, if he's not confident and not happy, then he's not going to perform.'

And what can a manager actually do about it?

> 'Well, the first thing is to be aware of it. To do that, you've got to monitor what goes on, and that means becoming friends with your players, getting close to them, gaining their trust. If they say to you: "Look, I've got a problem at home. It's my kid, or it's my wife, or it's a financial problem," or whatever, then you've got to try and help them. You've got to try and sort it out. It's not always easy, because they're not always so up front. Some keep things to themselves. Not everyone is the same. But I think having an "open door" policy, where players can come to you with their problems, is now universal among the managers that I know. Most clubs now employ an assistant manager, and he performs a very important role as a buffer or a conduit to the manager. If some managers retain a

certain authority and aloofness, it's not such a bad thing, as long as the players can approach his assistant, and speak to him through his assistant. Most modern managers, though, take a strong interest in what's happening in players' lives.'

Some of the greatest managers in the game were noted for building up an incredible amount of knowledge about their players, on and off the pitch. Jock Stein was known by the inhabitants of those parts of Glasgow where his players lived to do his own homework, generally outside office hours, to enable him to understand his players better. He would visit their families, he would frequent the pubs where they drank – and find out *how much* they drank. Supporters of Celtic were very happy to give him information, feeling, no doubt, that, far from spilling the beans on a player's habits behind his back, they were helping the manager to understand him better – which would spell better results on Saturday. If there were problems, Stein could nip them in the bud before they got too great. Big problems, after all, started out as small problems once.

With the job of manager becoming more complicated, and the additional responsibilities for financial decisions that most modern managers face, such scrutiny is less likely in the modern game. Even in Stein's era, his level of interest in 'the whole player' was probably exceptional. You can't help thinking, though, that if the extent of a player like Paul Merson's drinking and gambling had been known about earlier, it might not have reached the epic proportions that it did.

In football, as in business, a more consultative style of management is now accepted. It's no longer about telling all the time. 'Selling' an idea to a player can work more effectively, particularly if the player concerned is earning more than you are. Focusing exclusively on the job at hand will no longer work. You have to focus on the feelings of those in the team, too. That's not to say that you let the team make all the decisions for you, as some managers claim to have done – that could be taking player power too far. Nevertheless, players may want to contribute ideas of their own, and these may be very valuable. In days gone by, Tommy Docherty might have resented Terry Venables, then still a player at Chelsea, commanding more respect from the team than he did as a manager. More recently, one of the most memorable scenes from the documentary about Graham Taylor's reign as England manager, *An Impossible Job* (retitled *Do I Not Like That!* for the video market), concerns Taylor trying to explain a particular move to Paul Gascoigne. Gascoigne then tells Taylor how *he* would do it, and an instant clip shows the move leading to a goal. It's evidently not a bad idea to listen to your players occasionally. As for reward and punishment, the trend seems to be towards carrots rather than sticks if you want to avoid being labelled a turnip.

Film director and general big-mouth Michael Winner once defined teamwork as being hundreds of people all doing exactly what he told them. He never worked with the Honey Monster, though.

14: Your Country Needs You . . . But Do You Need Your Country?

'For the sake of peace and quiet, we hope England win no other sporting event until at least the middle of the next century. And even then, it's only the world whist championship.'

The Scottish edition of the *Sun*, 1992

Terry Venables' announcement that he intended to stop managing England when his contract ran out after the European Championship in the summer of '96 was treated by the papers as a shock roughly equivalent to that of the Queen announcing her immediate abdication on the grounds that she was planning to divorce Philip and marry Michael Jackson (please note that, in these turbulent times, all things are possible so if, by the time you read these words, this has already happened, bear in mind that it seemed unlikely at the time I typed it).

From my conversations with Terry over the previous year, however, I have to say it didn't come as quite that much of a surprise to me. I had always suspected that his plan had been to do the job he had been brought in to do to the best of his abilities and then move on. After all, the kudos of being England manager (or, to be technically accurate, Chief Coach) may make it seem more attractive than it really is. The post is presented as the pinnacle of one's achievements, the top of the tree, but is it really as attractive as it seems? Of course, there is all the press attention that goes with it, which might put some people off. But you get that if you manage a top league club, too. What about the intrinsic rewards of the job itself: are they as great as they seem?

'What the FA values in a coach is someone who can really get the best out of his players,' Terry told me. 'I believe I can do that very well, but to do it, you have to get to know the players well. At club level, say at Tottenham or at Barcelona, I was able to do that. I was able to follow their progress and be on the lookout for any problems day in, day out. For an international game, I get three days with the players before the match. How much use is that?'

Certainly for a manager whose reputation lies in assembling a committed and successful side through rapport with players, the England job – or any international job, come to that – is going to be a perennial source of frustration. Terry described an alternative approach:

> 'I spend a lot of time watching club matches on video, and this is very useful, particularly when you know the result in advance. For entertainment, of course, you'd rather not have the result in advance and have a bit of suspense. If you are looking to assess players, though, it's good to know the result and where the goals are going to come. It means you're much more aware of the subtle things leading up to a goal being scored or conceded. Getting to know the players as human beings is still missing, though. That's the real difficulty in international management. There simply isn't the time to do that, and I think most successful club managers would really miss it.'

I once ran into someone at work who had, many years previously, been an apprentice at Crystal Palace, where Terry had begun his coaching career. No one would have known in those days that El Tel would one day end up managing the national side, but was there anything about his style then that was particularly memorable, I wondered?

> 'The thing I'll always remember about Terry as a coach in those days was that he never once lost his temper with us. This doesn't mean that he didn't believe in discipline, but he was a very patient man. He would never shout at people or throw tea-trays around like some managers do. He wanted to instil a sense of self-belief in us, and if he were to get angry, our confidence would probably have been shaken quite badly at that age. So he never did. We always thought he was going to, that eventually something would happen and it would be the straw that broke the camel's back, but he surprised us. He never blew up.'

Not for Terry, then, the kidology adopted by some managers of bollocking a player in front of his team-mates or hurling a teacup so that it whistles past a player's ear before bouncing off the wall. Generally speaking, these tricks tend to work in the short term, but their impact soon fades. Psychologists know that when a certain action is continually punished, the effectiveness of that punishment begins to diminish. Terry's approach seems to centre much more on letting people be themselves rather than conditioning them to be what you want them to be. As Alan Smith pointed out earlier in this book, it's a style driven by the belief, however naive it may sound, that you are able to help players to improve, a belief Graham Taylor claims to have given up on during his time as manager of England. Such an approach inevitably takes time, time which, with the limited period an England manager can spend with his players, may simply not be available.

It is perhaps for this reason that an international manager will tend to pick players with whom he has already had an opportunity to build rapport and got to know inside out, not just as skilled sportsmen, but also as human beings. This may be irritating for the fan who wants to know why an on-form player from his own team hasn't been picked, in favour of someone the manager seems to 'know better'. However, picking players who you can read from top to bottom is not merely sentimental, though there is no doubt that such an approach puts great emphasis on loyalty – it seems perfectly rational, particularly when time to get to know others is scarce. Thus Venables' persistent faith in Gascoigne, where others might favour Le Tissier, is not unusual. It isn't a question of having favourites, it's a question of having players whose performance you can predict more effectively.

Many northern supporters feel that Terry 'always picks a bunch of Cockneys because he's one himself' – ex-Spurs players, in particular, which is interesting in view of the fact that Chairman Alan Sugar wouldn't let him in the stadium to watch them for a long time.

'Yeah, some people will say that,' Venables concedes. 'To be honest, though, I think I've always had even better rapport with players from the north-east, players like Peter Beardsley, Paul Gascoigne, Alan Shearer, Chris Waddle, Terry Fenwick . . .'

So there you have it: Terry is an honorary Geordie (admittedly, Chris Waddle used to support Sunderland, but then he's not in the side any more; and this is not the time to start a debate on the merits or otherwise of Terry Fenwick). Alas, Peter Beardsley did not make it to Terry's final squad for Euro '96. Maybe his age had counted against him. Ever the gentleman, Pedro took the news with quiet dignity. Lest there be any charges of favouritism, it should be noted that Scribes regular, Dennis Wise, also failed to make the final line-up.

Sometimes, when a player has not been picked for the England side, it has not been the decision of the England boss alone. It is not uncommon for the manager at the player's own club to advise against selecting him, particularly if he feels the player isn't suited to play from an emotional point of view. Fans can forget that if their favourite player doesn't make the side, their own club's boss might have had a say in the decision.

For Terry, the support of his friends is more important to his happiness than anything else. That's perhaps why, when the critics were carping in the papers and officials at the FA were refusing to give him wholehearted support he wanted, with court cases still to be fought and business partners having proved unreliable, he was still able to be totally relaxed and at ease, when he was with those he knows and trusts – and many players, past and present, fall into that category.

'What friends tell you is very important, and I take it seriously. The papers are doing their job, and sometimes that can hurt players, but I never let it get to me personally. The opinions of those you trust are what matters.'

Terry has documented the day-to-day highs and lows of his run-up to Euro '96 elsewhere, but his determination that he would not carry on after the tournament was very clear from the moment he announced it. Following a number of court cases he is determined to fight, I think we'll be seeing him back in his club management – though where remains a mystery for now. Sales of Linguaphone cassettes in the Kensington area, however, suggest he may be looking beyond these shores.

The weekend that the announcement was made that he would not be carrying on, I met him briefly. His usual ability to 'switch off' from the pressures of work on a Saturday night was clearly being stretched considerably, but he still had a smile on his face.

'Eventful week?' I asked him.

'About average,' he grinned back.

Like Terry, Scotland manager Craig Brown seems to possess the sense of humour vital to remain sane in the job. Unlike Terry, he was not a well-known club manager, prior to being appointed. Neither was his predecessor, Andy Roxburgh. Both, like Terry, had reputations for being particularly strong in coaching, and must again have experienced plenty of frustration at having so little time with the players to work on this.

With Scotland being smaller, it is possible that getting to know players is easier. Certainly, with most of the players chosen coming from a relatively small pool of big clubs, it must make things easier for your scouts. But it is probably still not a job that those successful in club management would have any burning need to pursue.

I asked Mark McGhee for his views. He had already made no secret of the fact that his ultimate ambition would be to go on to manage the most successful club on one or other side of the border (a former Celtic player admitting that ultimately he wouldn't mind a crack at managing Rangers must have given a few fans food for thought). But did his ambitions extend to international management?

'Manage Scotland? Not at this stage. Not at this stage.'

Nevertheless, he did qualify this thought . . .

'I think, if I had finished and had done everything I wanted to do here at Wolves – and there's an enormous amount I want to do and I think is possible here – and if I'd had enough of that, and they'd had enough of me . . . who's to say? I certainly would never say "never". But at this moment in time, it's not something that enters my mind.'

So, like fellow countryman Sean Connery, when it came to playing James Bond again, Mark was sticking to a philosophy of 'never say never'. But were the attractions of club management, with much more time to devote to the players and, let's not ignore it, generally more respectable salaries, inevitably greater than those of international management?

'Yes, I think that's absolutely true. I think, however, that maybe the experience of going to a World Cup with a team might be something to treasure. As a player, I won a couple of caps, but I never went to a World Cup, so I wouldn't mind experiencing that . . . but I think it's a long way into the future.'

Here we seem to have hit the nail on the head. From the point of view of any rational argument, a job managing a large club seems vastly more appealing than managing a national side. Indeed, when Terry announced he was leaving, many of the successful club managers were proposed by the newspapers as worthy successors, and many turned down the opportunity. As far as job satisfaction and salary are concerned, club management holds all the aces. And yet, and yet . . . Can winning even the European Cup compare with taking a national side all the way to winning the European Championship, or, even better, the World Cup? There is little doubt that, for the manager and players of the England team in 1966, nothing they ever did at club level could compare with the joy of winning that World Cup.

If you want to recruit an international manager, you should therefore aim at someone whose heart can rule their head, a manager who is fuelled by emotion, rather than reason.

Certainly, Terry Venables fits this mould. He says he is driven by what he feels is right, his own sense of justice. In his legal battles with opponents, it is a sense of emotion that keeps him fighting. A purely rational approach might be to cut your losses and pack up, but this is unlikely to cut much ice with Terry, and this same emotional conviction will tend to work for him in coaching the national team. The same is true of Craig Brown. Showing the players the film *Braveheart*, Mel Gibson's interpretation of the life of Scots hero William Wallace, prior to a vital Euro '96 qualifying game was a masterstroke. It's a film that appeals instantly to the emotions, rather than to detailed historical dissection, and, with its themes of honour, injustice, betrayal and integrity, is capable of stirring an English audience, let alone a Scottish one. The victory that followed was vital in securing Scotland a place in the final stages of Euro '96.

Interestingly, this move was very similar to one tried by Craig's predecessor, Andy Roxburgh, in the 1992 European Championships in Sweden. He had secured a copy of a television commercial which had stressed that landing on the moon, and the American space program in general, would not have been possible without a whole load of inventions made in Scotland. The advert had nothing to do with football, but plenty to do with pride and passion, and the Scots went on to slaughter the hotly fancied CIS team (what had been the USSR) 3–0. The sense of celebration, particularly considering England's dismal performance in that competition, could not have been rivalled, except perhaps immediately after the Battle of Bannockburn.

Passion and emotion are therefore the key. I was fascinated to find that a couple of the managers I had been interviewing were invited for interviews with the Irish Football Association for the job of managing the Republic of Ireland as successors to Jack Charlton. Charlton's reign had been a remarkable one, taking the team to the final stages of two World Cups, in Italy and in the States. To the fans, he was a saint, and this was all the more notable in view of the fact that there was nothing Irish about Big Jack at all. As honorary citizens go, Jack took some beating.

Again, what he instilled was emotion. When ex-player and prominent Irish journalist Eamon Dunphy started criticising the fact that his sides didn't do much in the way of passing, saying that his long-ball tactics were making him ashamed to be Irish, a bitter row broke out between gaffer and hack, with most Irish supporters taking Charlton's side, leaving Dunphy to slope off and start writing about U2 instead.

It wasn't that Dunphy's criticisms were unrealistic. That was just the point – they were all too realistic, and sensible, and carefully thought-out, and rational. Nobody wants that at international level. It's all very well, perhaps, with club management, where being realistic can be a bonus (interestingly, Charlton was never a particularly successful club manager), but when you're representing your country, or, in Jack's case, your adopted country, you need hopes and you need dreams. You need to dream the impossible dream and forget that your rational side is telling you it's impossible. Jack was superb at that. While he was manager, the whole country *believed.*

And, unlike poor Ally MacLeod, who had managed Scotland in '78, the country carried on believing, right until Jack left.

And so we come to talk of replacements. In the case of the new Irish manager, this was going to be no picnic. How do you replace a demigod?

Dave Bassett was one of the managers interviewed. At the time, he had left Sheffield United, the club where he had spent many years and which was now in a state of considerable flux and disarray, and had not yet signed for Crystal Palace, where he was to enjoy immediate success.

Perhaps, after the disheartening recent times in Sheffield, the novelty of international management had considerable appeal. Of course, 'Harry' wasn't Irish, but that had never stopped Jack. I found that Bassett disagreed that managing a national side is less satisfying than club management. Given that the financial rewards at a club like Sheffield United are unlikely to match those at, say, Newcastle or Manchester United, and given that the preceding months had not exactly been happy ones, it is easy enough to see why his views might have been thus.

'Certainly, it's a different emphasis,' he maintained. 'With club football, it's a week-in, week-out thing. Interest and coverage in the media and press doesn't stop. With managing a national side, it's more focused at particular times in the year. It's a different discipline.'

So, what of the fact that you have so much less time to spend with players than at club level?

'It's human nature. Whatever you haven't got, you want, don't you? If you're working with players every day, sometimes you think to yourself that you could do with a break! Then, when you don't see them so much, you want to see them more. That's the way it is. It's like your family. When you're with them all the time, you think "I could do with a break" and when you're not with them you find you didn't know how much you miss them.'

In the end, though, the job didn't go to Dave Bassett. It was, however, offered to one of his successors at Wimbledon, Joe Kinnear – who *turned it down!*

Joe had clearly agonised a bit over his decision. Wimbledon's position at the time was precarious, and losing a manager at that stage of the season would have done them no good at all. At the same time, the position of the Irish side wasn't looking all that promising, with most of the experienced players now getting on a bit, and unsettled and experimental times ahead. Rationally, it didn't seem a good move. Emotionally, however, for someone who has real Irish roots, it was a tough one to turn your back on and walk away.

Joe took the logical route. He let thinking guide feeling. His announcement that he had been very flattered, but that it had been 'the right job at the wrong time', gave a clue as to how he felt. He stayed with Wimbledon, the side that would otherwise probably have faced relegation, and in so doing, it seems, encouraged Vinnie Jones to pledge his future to the club, following an unsettled season.

The job went instead to Mick McCarthy, who had been manager of Millwall. Curiously, Millwall, like Wimbledon, had had a very strong start to the season, but were in a similar downward spiral at the time McCarthy left. By the end of the season, they had been relegated, and some tickets given to McCarthy had ended up in the hands of touts, adding further embarrassment. Cockney-hating fans in other parts of the country could at least take pleasure in the fact that this was likely to wipe the smile off Danny Baker's face for a couple of weeks, though an astute observer of the game like him had probably seen it coming a mile off.

McCarthy's start as manager of Ireland had been similarly unsuccessful. The results were dreadful, and promised little for the future. Assuming the fault wasn't a hundred per cent McCarthy's, Joe's decision not to take the job may well have been vindicated.

There but for the grace of God, as it were. On an emotional level, though, would he ever get such a chance again?

And talking of the grace of God brings us neatly on to Glenn Hoddle, to many a surprise choice as Terry Venables' replacement as England's Chief Coach a.k.a. manager. If, for Joe Kinnear, the offer of the Ireland job had come at the wrong time, for Glenn, the England job had come at what was arguably just the right time. The job might have a very strong down side, but, with all the bickering between director Matthew Harding and incomprehensibly driven chairman Ken Bates, so, it appeared, did Chelsea.

Glenn, a committed Christian, whose faith is central to his view of the game, and life in general, is certainly a manager for whom the emotional appeal of the top job is likely to outweigh any niggling objections on a rational level.

It's true that he is very young, but this is the trend these days, and youth can often bring a vitality and passion with it that can work wonders. A more serious objection might be that he has had relatively little experience as a coach. His achievements at Chelsea, while having endeared him to the fans, have amounted to one FA Cup final, which then fell rather flat, and middling results in the league, albeit executed with flair and creativity, winning plaudits from visiting fans.

Hoddle may be privately nervous about his lack of experience but, as we've established, this is no time to be rational.

The point is, you've got to believe, and for someone to whom faith is such a central tenet to his life, belief must come easily. He always had self-belief as a player, always sticking to a continental style. He had made big changes in the coaching methods at the club, and had been able to persuade a player of the calibre of the Dutch star Ruud Gullit (the fan's choice for Hoddle's replacement) to join the club. As if these weren't sufficient illustrations of his self-belief, let's face it, it must have taken some guts to sing a song as appalling as 'Diamond Lights' with Chris Waddle (not to be confused with Diamond White, a more attractive prospect altogether) and then allow it to be transmitted on *Top of the Pops*.

I honestly think that, if they were to think about it too deeply, *no one* would want to accept the England job. Furthermore, of the many names that were thrown around after Terry made his announcement, their results at club level were no better – in some cases rather worse – than those enjoyed by Glenn at Chelsea (think of Bryan Robson's Middlesbrough, Howard Kendall's Leeds, Ray Wilkins' QPR). No, I think in accepting a job like this, your heart *has* to rule your head, and while Joe Kinnear was able to rationalise his decision not to accept the Ireland job, Glenn hasn't let sober reason get in the way.

And anyway, who's to say that the pay isn't actually an improvement on what he could expect at Chelsea? Nothing would surprise me about them!

No, I think the boy's got potential. Like Jack Charlton, he can give the people something to believe in.

15: Trick or Cheat?

'All I learned at school
Was how to bend not break the rules . . .'

Madness

There is a seminal episode of *The Simpsons* in which Homer discovers that his daughter Lisa has the uncanny knack of being able to predict football results. It being the USA, they are unfortunately of the gridiron variety, rather than proper football results, but nevertheless prove very useful to Homer when it comes to laying bets on who will win what. This is illegal across most of the States as there are fears it would lead to people throwing matches (no chance of that over here, of course!) but if your daughter's got a gift like that, it seems a shame to waste it. An insight into how she does it comes when she gives her reasons behind picking three winners: one team is selected because its members are pure in heart, another because they're noble in spirit and a third – the LA Raiders, if I remember correctly – because they always cheat.

Wise words indeed. But there's cheating and there's cheating. Where is it unforgivable and where is it merely a bit of trickery, gamesmanship, psychological warfare or some such euphemism? How far can teams go towards bending the rules in their favour? And what are the attitudes of managers towards such chicanery? Does sleep not come, the whole night through, because your cheatin' heart's gonna tell on you – or do you laugh up your sleeve when you think you've pulled it off?

Everyone who has ever played football at any level will have stories of sneaky tactics designed to put opponents off their game ranging from inhospitable dressing rooms to non-stop banjo-playing outside a team's hotel room all night. How much does it go on at a professional level? I asked Mark McGhee . . .

'One thing I learned from my own experience is that Cambridge United used to go through a lot of routines designed to intimidate their opponents when they were warming up. They brought cones out on to the pitch as part of their pre-match routine. Also, when you arrived at Cambridge, there used to be no hot water, cold tea and for your own warm-up, the balls used to be the worst kicking balls you've ever seen in your life. It was definitely a psychological ploy to try and undermine our morale, and I think that sort of thing can affect you if you let it.

'When I went there with Reading, I was determined that it shouldn't affect us and I was also determined not to get sucked into making a big issue out of it. What I did do was to tell my players that after the warm-up, they should kick the balls as far out of the ground as they could possibly kick them! I then made sure that when they arrived at our place, there were cones there for them, that there were brand-new balls there for them to kick around, that they had everything they could possibly want to go through their own routines. So, rather than try to do to them what they did to us, I turned it round the other way – I went overboard the other way – and I found that was very much more effective.

'Everyone is always trying things like that all the time, that's for sure. A lot of managers don't give the teams out till very late. This is one Alex Ferguson would do when I played under him at Aberdeen: he used to have players who were

> injured and not going to play stepping in and out of the dressing room, wearing the kit, or just popping their heads round the door asking if someone could fetch them something. That way, the opponents would see an injured player in a jersey prior to the team sheet going up and think that he must be playing, but then, of course, he wasn't! Anything you can do to win a game is worth doing.'

There is no doubt that, in the case of Alex Ferguson, old habits die hard. When it comes to psychological warfare, he's still your man, many years later. Is it really 'playing the game', though? Kevin Keegan obviously thought otherwise.

Towards the end of the 1995–96 season, the race for the Championship in the Premier League had, despite Liverpool's best efforts, become a two-horse one between Newcastle and Manchester United. Newcastle, having been at the top for most of the season, had been overtaken by Man U, and, despite having games in hand, were clearly under greater pressure, the bookies tipping the Manchester side for the title. Against this backdrop, manager Ferguson began what looked to most observers like an incredibly sneaky war of words and process of psychological intimidation designed to scupper any chances Newcastle might have had. It took the form of taunting their opponents along the lines that they were bound to play less well against Newcastle, because they were keener that the black-and-whites should beat Man U to the title, thereby wounding the opponents' sense of pride and making them play more effectively, or, conversely, claiming that sides tried much harder against his own team than against others, thereby attacking their sense of fair play.

Specifically, he seemed to suggest that Leeds United, who had played extremely well against his side (but still lost), had only done so out of some spoilsport attempt to stop Man U winning the League and wouldn't expend nearly as much effort against Newcastle. He claimed that, had he been managing Leeds, he would have felt let down that the side didn't play the way they did against Man United all season: 'On that performance, they should be a top six team. They're not. They're struggling, so they've been cheating their manager. Leeds play Newcastle next, and I would like to see a video of that one.' He went on to taunt Nottingham Forest along similar lines, with dark hints about Newcastle being invited there for Stuart Pearce's testimonial game shortly after the season was finished, and drawing attention to the fact that Forest manager Frank Clark was himself a Geordie. The implication was clear: the Nottingham team would lie down and let Newcastle walk over them, while pulling out all the stops to defeat Man U.

Lest anyone think that these were just words taken out of context and reinterpreted by a press keen to maximise any tension between the two clubs at the top, it is worth bearing in mind Mark McGhee's words about Ferguson at Aberdeen: *Anything you can do to win a game is worth doing*.

Scottish fans will have further recollections of gamesmanship from Ferguson's Aberdeen days. One classic was the abandoned-set-piece-which-isn't-really-abandoned-after-all routine, involving such stars as Gordon Strachan. Here, two players would simultaneously go for a free kick, appear to make a complete pig's ear of it, and just when Aberdeen's opponents were relaxing, thinking that the kick would be taken again, one or other of the players would do a swift about-turn, gaining possession of the ball in doing so, and make a run for glory before the other side knew what had hit them.

No cheeky bit of opportunism this, you can't help thinking. A move like that has to be *rehearsed!* Of course, it's not the kind of thing you can get away with for ever, but they'll tell you in a hundred Scottish pubs that this particular stunt worked its magic more than once.

It is in the war of words, however, that Ferguson is perhaps most clearly in his element. Of course, some might argue that none of it is a deliberate attempt to wind up other sides at all, it is just a reflection of Man U's 'us against the world' siege mentality and general sense of persecution, a paranoia that hasn't quite reached the clinical stage, but is getting there. One does not necessarily preclude the other, though. Indeed, the 'everyone's out to get us' conspiracy-theory mentality (and, let's face it, apart from the side's own supporters, everyone *does* hate Man United), may be what starts the plotting and the scheming and the psychological warfare in the first place.

Certainly, one person who didn't think it was fair was Kevin Keegan. Generally an easy-going and apparently relaxed manager, he exploded at Ferguson's comments on live television, suggesting that Leeds should send him the video he wanted (Newcastle beat them, but they had fought hard, apparently fired up by the remarks made against them) and describing Ferguson's observations as 'close to being slanderous'. His emotional reaction – apparently near to tears – recalled his loss of control as a player, many moons before, when he and Leeds' Billy Bremner had received their marching orders. Such situations have been so rare in Keegan's time in football that there was little doubt how much Ferguson's words had affected him.

But who won in the end? 'I guess you'd have to say that Ferguson did!' pointed out Jim Smith. The public sympathy may have been with the human, vulnerable Keegan who had let it all spill out, but unfortunately, the shrewd, machiavellian Ferguson went on to win the Championship.

In the years to come, people will no doubt look back on the whole exchange as they do now at Maradona's goal scored from a handball against England in the 1986 World Cup in Mexico. He'd called it 'The Hand of God' and the fans had called him a cheating bastard, but now they tend to look back more philosophically. After all, his other goal in the same match had been one of impeccable craftsmanship, so Argentina probably would have won anyway. It's best not to dwell on these things. Although, the Germans still gripe about whether the ball really crossed the line in '66!

And then came Mexico '70, and more gamesmanship, as the honking horns and the playing of loud music kept the England team awake in their hotel and ill-prepared for the match that was to follow.

According to Mark McGhee: 'You get away with a lot more at international level because of differences in language and culture than you do in a domestic situation, where everyone tends to do the same things and have the same privileges.'

When he was playing for Celtic, Mark McGhee was part of the team that played against Dynamo Kiev and brought along their own food, together with a chef from Glasgow's Grosvenor Hotel to prepare it for them. The reason? The Chernobyl nuclear power plant had blown up just around the corner, and the team were taking no chances. You have to say, though, that blowing up a power station next to your stadium beats honking a few car horns outside the team hotel by a long shot. Let's be charitable, and say it was an accident.

What about bringing in people like hypnotists to give his team an edge – is this something Mark would try?

> 'Nothing quite as bizarre as that, but I am very interested in specialists. Anyone who can enhance performance by any means is worth listening to. I think that, like with other things, different people are affected in different ways by different techniques so I don't think one single thing really works carte blanche. You've got to give players the option, really, by saying: "I'm thinking of introducing something new – do you think that would help you?" Doing it that way is much better than saying: "Right – we're all going to be hypnotised!" or "We're all going to take seaweed!" If you want to take seaweed and you think it'll help you, then take it. There is a lot of good to be had in employing people with specialist knowledge, definitely. Nowadays, managers' coaching budgets allow them to diversify a bit and to bring in a few specialists.

It allows a wee bit of diversity in your coaching and the chance to work on individual players' inadequacies and weaknesses and build on other players' strengths.'

Alan Smith has certainly been prepared to try different schemes designed to give his teams an advantage:

'It can be a help, because I believe that working in a football club is very much like working in a submarine, where you're submerged underwater for thirty-nine weeks of the year, and you do get a bit touchy. It's not like the travelling salesman who's out of the office some days. You go to the same training ground every day, you travel on the same coach every day, share the same changing rooms . . . these are all very small, confined areas and it's very difficult to avoid getting a bit touchy – and a bit tetchy – with one another, so anything to break out of that routine and try something new helps.

'So I've done all those things you hear about. I've done *everything!* I've tried go-karting, taking them out to army camps, taking them to Chinese restaurants, just to get them out for the night, taking them away for three days here, two days there . . .'

All this sounds perfectly acceptable in the pursuit of team-building. What about the more unusual stuff?

'Oh, yes! I've had "sports psychoanalysts" in the last year and I brought in that hypnotist guy, Paul McKenna.'

McKenna, in addition to encouraging seemingly normal people to waltz around with mops or making truck drivers think they're ballerinas on television, has a lucrative sideline in tapes, both audio and video, designed to help relax you through hypnosis and make you more focused on the skills involved in a particular sport. Heartily endorsed by the likes of boxer Nigel Benn (his techniques being condemned as 'cheating' by indignant opponent Chris Eubank), some of his tapes deal specifically with football. So how did he go down with the players at Palace?

> 'He went down well for a bit, except when he couldn't do it any more and he passed it on to his assistant. They didn't like his assistant, because he didn't have the same snob value as Paul McKenna, although he was doing exactly the same thing.'

So that was that, then. If the same had happened to Nigel Benn, we'd probably still have to endure Chris Eubank winning everything!

> 'Then I brought in another "sports psychoanalyst", who ended up trying to take me and the team over, almost! He wanted to get involved in the training and in the way we do our warm-ups. He sent me a huge bill, which was ridiculous. You start off with good intentions like that, and then it starts to run away with you. This guy caused me a lot of problems. He's a South African guy, and I got him initially through a journalist. Dave Bassett had used him, although I didn't know that at the time. I got him in and he hung about the training ground a lot, and he was hanging about a lot of the time while I was having the problems with Chris Armstrong failing the drugs test, going along to the Liverpool cup tie and so on. Then he started to query what I did, saying that I spent far too much time with the press, and started analysing me, and it all got very heavy. Then he tried to claim about fifteen thousand pounds off the club for the work he'd done and it all got very bitter. So what started out as a good idea turned sour.
>
> 'I have to say, though, that when he first came in he had an

impact, and I find that's true of a lot of these people. They start by making a difference, but after the second, third and fourth sessions, that starts to wane away very much. I've become a bit anti all that now. I do have some players at Wycombe who I feel could do with some analysing, because they don't have enough confidence in their ability and are better than they think they are. You get that with the younger players – they've all got hang-ups. There's no one in life, I'd imagine, who hasn't got some sort of hang-up, whether it's the size of one's nose, the lack of one's hair, the feeling that your wife doesn't love you or whatever. So everyone needs some psychological help, no matter how self-confident they are, and I've got three players at my club at the moment who I believe would benefit from having someone sit down with them and talk through what the problem is, but I'm put off by my experiences at Palace. While I was there, I must have employed four or five different people at different times and with all of them, there ended up being a problem.'

Does this simply reflect the quality of people setting themselves up as experts in this area?

'It's happened with them all. With Paul McKenna, when he came in, it was all very much the same. We never seemed to step up or make any progress. The same happened with another guy I brought in, whose specialist area was sports fitness. He did a certain amount of analysing and again it started off all right, *but* . . .

'It's a shame, because I believe there *is* a place for it, but within the confines of a football club, and the confines of time, it can be quite difficult to fit it in – and it *shouldn't* be, because we don't work enough hours! That's the illogical part of it. When you get knocked out of a cup competition, as we were this year out of the FA Cup and the Autoglass

Whatever, you find yourself with time on your hands, but of course you wouldn't have that time if you were still in those competitions, so you can't book it out.

'In the end, the best psychologist a team has should be the manager himself.'

And indeed, the best managers were generally excellent amateur psychologists. Stories abound, apocryphal or otherwise, of the great managers of yesteryear and their 'kidology', playing on a player's weakness here, exploiting a chink in a player's personality there . . . which reminded Alan Smith:

'Well, from what I hear at Wycombe, my predecessor Martin O'Neill spent a lot of his time playing mind games with the players. He didn't coach them. Some of the things he did seem ridiculous to me, but it was obviously a mind-game approach that he had. There was method in his madness.'

Judging from what Martin O'Neill was able to do at Leicester later on in the season, you have to agree!

'In the end, though, I think those tricks run a bit thin. Dave Bassett seems to me to be the classic example of that. I've known David for years. My first coaching job was at Wimbledon, when Bassett was a player there. He introduced me to the club and got me my job there. His methods influenced me and some of the things he tried – the army camps and the go-karting nights and so on – do help, but he was always very strong-minded, and because he had come from outside professional football, also very open-minded.'

True enough. At Sheffield United, Dave Bassett brought in motivation gurus and even had a sports psychologist, Dr Andy Cale, on the books for a couple of seasons.

> 'But the truth is that when he hasn't had very good players, he hasn't done very well either. He got Watford relegated, Sheffield United he's taken up and then down again. It's hard to do with less strong-minded players. And is his mind that strong now? He's – what? – fifty-one, fifty-two? He's had outside interests and has always been a bubbly, buoyant character, but you have to ask yourself whether events have taken their toll on him. The painful way that Sheffield United were relegated the season before last – you just don't know how much that takes out of people. I was at that match at Stamford Bridge. That can hit you very hard.'

As it was, however, both Dave Bassett and Martin O'Neill were to have unexpectedly good seasons, of which more anon.

In the end, it is up to the reader to decide which of the examples quoted here are gamesmanship and good psychology and which are a bit beyond the pale. Kevin Keegan has made his views on manipulative public statements very well known. No one has been particularly outspoken about the place of hypnosis in football. As for sports psychologists and specialist dietitians, most would agree that these are probably fair enough – the problem comes when they start wanting to take over the manager's job.

Cheating, like anything else, is in the eye of the beholder to some extent, but with fortunes now riding on the winners and losers as football changes, there are going to be a few arguments in pubs about definitions of fair play and the grey line between what is acceptable psychological trickery and what is thoroughly unsportsmanlike behaviour.

As for Alex Ferguson, I know I speak for the entire population of Tyneside, when I express the hope that his cheatin' heart will make him weep. You don't have to cheat to be a winner.

But it certainly seems to help.

16: Two-Horse Race

'Closer . . . closer!'

Hannibal Lecter, *The Silence of the Lambs*

For those who like a close contest (and, if we're honest, most of us would probably prefer a runaway victory for our own side), the 1995–96 season was shaping up very well indeed. South of the border, Liverpool were making a comeback after a poor start and Stan Collymore, despite remaining someone Alan Smith wouldn't pay to see perform, unlike Shirley Bassey, had begun to adopt a less self-centred mentality, which was paying rich dividends. No longer was he an out-and-out striker seeking to score as many goals for himself as he possibly could. Roy Evans' masterstroke in teaming him up with Robbie Fowler formed a sparkling combination. Collymore still scored individual goals, but was perhaps most effective at laying them on for his striking partner. The player whom Alan Smith had never believed would attain the maturity needed to succeed in the Premiership was adapting, learning and finally coming good.

At Manchester United, despite Andy Cole only ever being able to find his goal touch for the odd, but generally crucial, goal, things were still progressing well, with a new, calm, bald Eric Cantona providing continued inspiration and supersub Paul Scholes making a name for himself as one of several players who, as in the

Liverpool side, combined talent with youth.

Newcastle were blazing the trail and, for supporters like me, allowed us to believe that this time there would be no slip-ups and the Championship would be ours (hindsight is the enemy of such innocence, but it was good while it lasted). We appreciated Asprilla, even if no one else did, and late signing David Batty proved invaluable (that vital little slip against Forest aside – God, it's painful typing this).

As the remaining days of the season ticked away, this three-horse race was gradually whittled down to two, Liverpool's lack of early form having come back to haunt them, and it was between the two Uniteds until that final match, when everything went black. Sorry, sorry, I must keep my objectivity.

That was the picture in England, too close to call until very near the end, giving plenty to talk about, even for neutral supporters.

In Scotland, it was very open, too. All season it had been a two-horse race between Rangers and Celtic. And, on the evidence of the previous few years, that was one horse more than usual.

For the first time in ages, Celtic were mounting a serious challenge to Rangers' recent supremacy. Rangers' goal of beating the nine Championships that Celtic had once won in a row (before the arrival of chairman David Murray had allowed the Rangers renaissance) was going to be made more difficult by Tommy Burns' boys – indeed Bhoys – at the newly rebuilt stadium they called Paradise. Another Championship win for Rangers would bring their total to eight in a row – tantalisingly close to Celtic's historical record ('Eight would be great, nine would be fine, but ten would be ten in a row!' was one ditty adopted by the fans).

After poor performances in European competition for both clubs, how had this affected their managers' resolve and what impact would it have on the Championship race?

For Walter Smith, Rangers manager and in pole position with Celtic snapping at his heels, the European embarrassment had been greater, because expectation had been higher. Rangers supporters had been well used to winning domestic honours and were now looking further afield.

'What happened in the European Cup, or the "Champions' League", did affect the morale of the players in a way, but I encouraged us to look at it as rationally as we could. We played Borussia Dortmund, the champions in Germany, and Steaua Bucharest, who are two *very* high-standard teams. We drew with Borussia Dortmund twice, we lost in the last couple of minutes in the game in Bucharest and then we drew one–one with them. There were no great differences in performance between ourselves and either of those two sides. We were very much on a par with them. Now neither ourselves nor the other two could compete with Juventus this year. Now, we have to look at that realistically and say that Juventus had made it quite clear that winning the European Cup was their one aim this season. Their whole motivation was geared towards that, and their manager was quite open about it – he told everyone that that was what they were aiming for, that they didn't think they were going to win the Italian League, so the European Cup was the big one, as far as they were concerned.

'Well, we caught them right in the middle of the section and we were quite soundly beaten by them. Yes, I did have to sit down and spell out a few home truths to the boys over that one. We didn't hide from it, or walk away from it. We were well beaten in that game – in both the Juventus games – but I was able to point out that those games were perhaps not typical of European standards, that we had acquitted ourselves well against the other two teams, and that we'd had two or three victories in this year's campaign, rather than none at all, which had been the case last season. We didn't try to make excuses for our performance against Juventus – there *were* no excuses, as we'd been soundly beaten.

'Some other good sides didn't progress far in the tournament this year, though, and for us, the main motivation is always to win another championship here in Scotland and keep adding to our record in an attempt to beat Celtic's. We have to make sure that that's our main motivation for every season. That wasn't the case with Juventus, the Italian League being much more open. They'd spent some time building up a good side, they'd won the Italian League for the first time in twelve seasons or so, and now they could afford to focus everything on winning the European Cup. Borussia Dortmund and Steaua Bucharest, like us, also wanted to do well in their domestic leagues, and try to win them. That's been the most realistic chance of success for all three of us.'

Was the fact that Celtic were putting up a real challenge this season unsettling to a team used to having things their own way for so long, or was the increased competition helping?

'Oh, definitely the latter. You only have to look at the record. By mid-February, we have lost only two games, whereas we'd lost five at the same point the previous season.'

In fact, Rangers were only to lose three games in the season altogether!

'We were already well ahead of our rivals by that time last year, though – despite not having played as well as this season – and I think we won the League Championship with five games to go! This year, we've had Celtic, who are our biggest rivals in every sense, chasing us hard, and it's making us play better, so that's been good for both clubs. The rivalry hasn't been causing any great nerves, but it has stimulated and pushed us on to better performances this season than last.'

Has this meant a different approach this season, telling the players different things and concentrating on other priorities, compared to what had gone on before when the club was so far ahead of the pack?

'No, not really. I'd like to think that my approach was more or less the same. I'm sure the players realise the change in situation themselves. They know that Celtic have the Championship in their sights and have the wherewithal to continue their run, which distinguishes them from the smaller clubs who don't have Celtic's backing and tend to have more trouble going into the latter stages of the season. The players can tell this for themselves. There's no need to keep reminding them that Celtic will be staying with us all the way. In fact, I don't think it's a good idea to highlight that fact any more than is necessary! The fact that we've now won seven Championships in a row is something that Rangers has never achieved before, and we'd obviously like to make it eight. Everyone is aware that Celtic were able to do nine in a row, and that's something that everyone here at Ibrox would like to emulate. It's very much a motivating factor.'

Despite the success, Rangers continued to buy players as the season went on. Is this a good idea, or is there a danger of unsettling the side? (Witness the misgivings many expressed when Kevin Keegan bought Faustino Asprilla for Newcastle late on in the season and altered Newcastle's style of play to accommodate him.)

'It's more difficult these days to maintain a settled side. I don't believe that selling and bringing in new players is always necessarily your choice. It may seem that way to the general public a lot of the time, but, in the case of Rangers, we had a lot of players who were reaching the end of their careers and it was just a natural thing to try and replace them. When you look around at all the major clubs, though, in Britain especially, there has been a lot of movement of players. Look at Manchester United at the beginning of the season, selling players like Mark Hughes and Paul Ince, who you felt were an integral part of the team. I think that is going to become part and parcel of football in the future at every club.'

One of the reasons for this, according to Walter, has been the case concerning Jean-Marc Bosman, a Belgian player who successfully took the club that employed him to the European Court of Justice over the circumstances of his transfer. RFC Liège had demanded a transfer fee for him from France's US Dunkerque, despite the fact that he had reached the end of his contract, and refused to sell him because of suspicions about the French club's ability to pay. Bosman won his case, not only against his former club, but also against the Belgian Federation and even UEFA. It was a landmark case which essentially established that any claims a club tries to have on a player, following the end of his period of contract, are contrary to European law. Many saw this as a severe blow to clubs and a victory for the players-as-individuals school of thought, more popular with agents like Eric Hall and Paul Stretford.

'I don't think that, in the light of the Bosman ruling, we're going to see the stability of teams that we've grown used to maybe ten or twenty years ago,' Walter told me.

Has this led to a change in players' attitudes, observable at Rangers?

'It's not apparent yet, but it will be. There will be a very heavy burden of transfer fees placed on clubs that wish to get their services. It's very likely that players will find themselves enticed away from a club where they would previously have spent, perhaps, ten years. They'd leave after maybe three or four. It is going to be a big concern for the larger clubs like ourselves and we'll all have to get used to more mobility of players.'

Won't it just mean that clubs will have to tempt players into signing longer-term contracts?

'I don't think so, because players themselves will be loath to sign long-term contracts. The clubs might like it that way, but the players just won't want to sign contracts that are too long. I think you'll be lucky to see four-year contracts being signed.'

Perhaps this instability and the need for revolving doors on players' entrances, as they come and go faster than ever before, will get in the way of grabbing those elusive ten Championships in a row. Everyone in Scotland who doesn't support Rangers is probably hoping so.

Both Rangers and Celtic were now buying more continental players than ever before. Did this present unique problems for those players settling in?

'In the football sense, probably no more so than players from other clubs. There is always a little time needed for a new player to settle in, get to know the other players around him, get to know the club's coaching style. There is the language difficulty, sometimes, and, while there is seldom much problem from the point of view of playing – a player with ability can fit in easily – outside the game, there may be more problems blending into society in general than you would find with, say, an English player coming to play up here. There's settling in, housing-wise and all those things, and they can take a little longer if you don't speak the language.

'These difficulties are sometimes exaggerated, though. We've certainly had our fair share of continental players and we've only had one or two who have had any difficulty settling in and haven't enjoyed playing for the club. Even a player like Paul Gascoigne, coming from Italy, may take a little time to re-adjust, but as players have more and more freedom to move abroad, I think we'll be seeing a lot more of their influence.'

Meanwhile, at Celtic, Tommy Burns was managing the side that had posed the greatest threat to Rangers' continued supremacy in recent years. European competition had again proved a disappointment, with a heavy defeat by Paris St Germain in the Cup Winners' Cup, but again the manager was being philosophical about it:

'I think that, from our point of view, facing that particular team came a little bit early for us. I'd like another crack at them right now! But it was early on to be facing a team of such quality – though it was a great experience. A great experience for the players, the supporters and myself.'

Even so, it must have been very disappointing on the night. How does a manager turn it into something positive, from which his players can benefit?

'Basically, it's all down to what you can learn from the team you're playing against, with regard to the whole team as a unit and also the individuals within that unit: how they move the ball, pass the ball, make themselves available for the ball; how they go forward and then back again; how they slow down the tempo of the game and then speed it up, depending on what area of the field they're in. Lots of little things like that.'

As in Rangers' case, there seemed to be very little hangover effect from defeat in this competition. Domestic performance seemed unaffected.

'No, there was no great hangover. We knew that we'd come up against a team that was better than us, but we felt that we'd carry on doing what we were doing, as we were getting quite far down the road of becoming a good little ball-playing and passing team ourselves. We got a good lesson that night in showing us how far we've still to go, but to be fair to the players, they've come a long way since that, as well.'

What has been the big difference this season, compared to last, during which, despite winning the Scottish FA Cup and being runners up in the Scottish League Cup (the Skol Cup), the club had not posed a serious threat to their rivals in the chase for the League Championship?

'Last year, we were a sort of mix-and-match team, with players who we were seeing how well they could do over a period of time, players we were wanting to let go and players that we were hoping to bring in, so it was very much a transitional period, whereas this season we've been much more settled. The team itself has rarely changed.'

There seemed to be less fluctuation in Celtic's line-ups, compared to their rivals, Rangers.

'When you see a lot of changes happening in a team then, more often than not, injuries have a lot to do with it. If you have a lot of them, then you have to chop and change all the time, but if you don't, then you want to try and get a settled team – your strongest team – and that's what you go with.'

Celtic have always had a tradition of concentrating very strongly on youth policy, too.

'Yes, we had a fantastic result against the Rangers youth team, the under-eighteens, who were beaten five–nil here at Celtic Park. The quality of our young players was there for all to see. Below them, at the sixteen-year-old level, we've got another group of fantastic young players, so I feel we're building the club along the right lines. Having been to Ajax, and seen how successfully their youth policy works, we're very keen to do exactly the same here at Celtic.'

This faith was to be vindicated towards the end of the season, as Celtic's junior players won the BP Youth Cup. Repercussions of the Bosman ruling permitting, the club was assembling a formidable side for the future.

With Celtic enjoying tremendous support, a support which remained strong even before Tommy's arrival, when the club was going through a bad patch, how difficult would it be to deliver what the fans expected? Were their expectations unrealistic? In contrast to earlier in the season, when he had produced a more cautious response to a similar question, the manager's confidence in his team had clearly increased beyond even his own expectations:

'Whatever the fans hope for, we want to deliver that. We want to give the fans everything that they've wanted. We'll do our very best to do that. I think we have played faster than I would have anticipated at the beginning of the season, and I believe that's down to the determination and the attitude of the players.'

Giving so much credit to the players is typical of Burns' approach. There is definitely a sense of 'family' about the club with him in charge of the team. The only manager I spoke to for this book who tended to play down his own role and play up that of the players to an equivalent extent was Frank Murphy at non-league Dulwich Hamlet, coincidentally a big Celtic fan himself.

Clearly, however, there would only be one winner this season and, as the weeks passed, you might have expected that the tension would mount among the players.

I was therefore interested to read about a study carried out by Dr Howard Kahn, a Scottish psychology lecturer, who had interviewed 512 players and ten managers, and had found that the players experienced very little stress indeed! Compared to most other jobs, players in Scotland seemed hardly to worry about anything. This was put down to the fact that the vast majority are not actually expecting to win anything, so there's very little pressure on them.

What of Celtic and Rangers though? Could it be that they felt under no pressure because they were so determined that they *would* win something? I suspect that a lot would have hinged on how late in the season the sampling was done. At the beginning of the season, anything seems possible. It is only towards the end that this attitude ceases to be a realistic one and stress is likely to begin biting.

Who bears the brunt of the stress, then? The managers, naturally. The survey confirmed this. I think the final month or so of the season would have been a tough one for both Walter Smith and Tommy Burns.

Rangers beat Celtic in the semi-finals of the Scottish FA Cup. As far as Tommy Burns was concerned, there was only the Championship to play for, and that too seemed to be slipping slowly out of reach.

Meanwhile, the issues discussed here turned out to have considerable bearing on the result of the European Cup Final, as, sure enough, Juventus, who had thrown all their efforts into winning this competition, were to emerge triumphant after a penalty shootout, beating an Ajax side with several of its stars bound for pastures new, following the Bosman ruling. Juventus were focused, while Ajax seemed disjointed and unstable. With the implications of the ruling for star players, it is lucky that Ajax have such an effective youth policy to nurture new talent.

As far as Celtic and Rangers are concerned, the fans of the two clubs are likely to remain poles apart for ever, but increasingly the spirit of animosity between these two faces of what was once the second city of the Empire seems to be diminishing. Several of the players socialise and have even been interviewed together in magazines, while the managers seem to have a respect for one another which didn't exist under previous regimes.

Tommy Burns commented during one interview: 'We have to move away from being derogatory and vitriolic about one another. I have nothing but respect for Walter Smith and Rangers, what they have done and the quality of the players they have, like Gascoigne. We've done well, but they've done better – for the moment.'

Ah, yes. For the moment. Celtic's talented youngsters are getting older and, as Liverpool and Manchester United have shown, talented youngsters can be the basis of very effective teams. I have no doubt that Celtic will continue to give Rangers a run for their money, and Rangers will continue to keep looking over their shoulders for the moment when Celtic overtake them. Time will tell if Rangers get their nine in a row – or even ten – or if this two-horse race will finish with Celtic ahead by a nose. Maybe more horses will get up to speed in the future, making the Bell's Scottish Premier League even more exciting, and shifting a few more wee drams for United Distillers.

One thing is likely – it's getting so close, it could need a photo finish.

17: Looking Back, Over My Shoulder

'My soul slides away
But don't look back in anger
I heard her say
(At least not today).'

Noel Gallagher

In one magazine interview, the songwriter from Oasis quoted above found himself talking about this song, one which sounds more like the Beatles did than even the Beatles do nowadays. He said that just as Liverpool's Kop used to echo to 'She Loves You Yeah, Yeah, Yeah', so he imagined the newly revamped Kippax at Manchester City sadly singing as the club got relegated: 'Don't look back in anger . . .'

It didn't happen quite like that, though Oasis did play Maine Road towards the end of the season and, shortly afterwards, Manchester City were indeed relegated. The side was the last confirmed relegation from the Premier League, Queen's Park Rangers and Bolton Wanderers having already known of their fate the previous week. Ironically, it was against Liverpool that Manchester City played their final match, when they managed to turn the result around from being two-nil down to a two all draw. Unfortunately, it wasn't enough. Another goal would have saved them, but the team was unable to score it. It was a terrible way to go down, but there is never a pleasant way to experience the drop from the top flight. I have already written of Dave Bassett's feelings when he experienced last-minute-of-the-season relegation with Sheffield United – probably the most devastating moment of his football career.

City fans, whose fondness for Oasis reciprocated the band's fondness for the football club, had been used to the team coming on to the pitch to the tune of the hit 'Roll With It', and had even adapted the words of another favourite, 'Wonderwall', to turn it into an anthem about their manager: 'And after all, you're my Alan Ball'. The song had grown and evolved to include praise of the season's wonderboy, Georgi Kinkladze, a world-class player if ever I saw one, but one excellent player doesn't make a successful team (Southampton, over-reliant as ever on Matt Le Tissier, only just survived). 'Maybe, you're gonna be the one that saves me' ran the lyric. Alas, it was not to be.

I resisted phoning Alan Ball at the end of the season, despite the fact that he had earlier said that he might be available. I had taken the 'might' to hinge on City's final position, and no normal person would like to be interviewed under such circumstances. There would, nevertheless, be plenty of journalists queuing up to ask how relegation felt. It doesn't take a psychologist to know the answer to that one. It's like those news reporters asking families how they feel about their houses having just burnt down.

Having several friends and colleagues who support the relegated teams made my own disappointment that Newcastle didn't win the Championship seem rather slighter by comparison. Nevertheless, it was a bittersweet time all round. More bitter than sweet, if truth be told.

There is no doubt that the end of the season is a bad time for most managers, too. Managers who had, during the early part of the season, been bursting with optimism and high hopes, now closed ranks, stopped talking and started disappearing on last-minute shopping trips for players or emergency team camps.

Terry Venables had some advice about this: 'Just go to all the managers who are still optimistic this season. They'll still be happy to talk . . .'

But just who were these remaining optimists?

'Oh, the ones at the top: Kevin Keegan; Alex Ferguson; Roy Evans . . .'

Alas, I suspect that, even at the top, optimism might have been in rather short supply. After all, despite the openness of the season being greater than in the past, by the end only one of these would be laughing and, given the nature of the individual concerned, probably not for all that long.

As Mark McGhee had already pointed out: 'There's only one team that wins the cup and there are only four teams that win a championship in a season, so out of the ninety-two or however many it is teams that there are, only four or five can be successful, and all the others have, in some ways, failed. Football managers are especially vulnerable to the disappointment of that.'

Well, there are a couple of other cups at one level or another, and other teams get promoted, so that's something to shout about, but beyond that, it's a fairly accurate assessment. The end of the season is bound to be a huge disappointment for the vast majority of managers, players and fans. Particularly if some clubs will insist on winning leagues *and* cups, thereby leaving less to go round for everyone else.

For supporters of Manchester United in England and Rangers in Scotland, there was plenty to celebrate. Both clubs won the double, coming top of their respective Premier Leagues and winning their respective FA Cups. For most other supporters, it was misery all round.

Walter Smith was even-tempered as ever in victory. Just as defeat by Juventus in the European Champions' League had been something that he had refused to let bring him down too much, so victory was not something he gloated about. He had done his job well and, if the European blow had been something of an embarrassment, so winning both domestic honours had been a vindication of his abilities. He had experienced more of a challenge this year from Tommy Burns' resurgent Celtic, already busy extending the size of their stadium further in the close-season. Next year would be harder still, but you could rely on his legendary calmness to see him through. Whether Rangers would, the following year, equal Celtic's record of nine Championships in a row and perhaps overtake it, or whether the important psychological factor that their record was about to be reached would yet spur Celtic to spoil the party was something only time would tell. The signing of Paul Gascoigne, criticised by many journalists at the time as a risky move, given the star's fitness, had been one of Walter Smith's best decisions, but other players – notably Brian Laudrup – had also been devastatingly effective. Gascoigne won the award for Scottish Player of the Year, proving once again that the gulf between the Jocks and the Geordies is in the eye of the beholder.

Tommy Burns praised Rangers' performance and acknowledged that they had been the better team . . . for the time being. Like Arnold Schwarzenegger, he'd be back.

Given that the highs in the game occur comparatively rarely (except for clubs like Rangers and Manchester United), it is important to savour them to the full, whether you are a manager or a player. After all, in this game, you're only as good as your last triumph (and in many clubs' cases, that was before most of the supporters were born). Victory is fleeting. *Sic transit gloria mundi*, and all that.

Mark McGhee fully agrees: 'Today's news is tomorrow's chip paper, you know. Things move and things change quite quickly in this game. Any season's Champions should enjoy every minute of it, because come August it's all over and they're at it again, the race is back on. So the players and the club itself should milk it until then, and get everything that they can get out of it.'

How true. Looking back at the previous season, when Blackburn were Champions, it all now seems so very long ago. Even by the time you read this, many of the incidents mentioned in this book will have begun to recede into the backs of people's minds as fresh incidents, similar in theme but very different in specifics, come to prominence. Andy Warhol's prediction that in the future everyone would be famous for fifteen minutes was rarely truer than in the football world. So polish that silverware and display it prominently before someone else gets their hands on it. Savour the hyperbolic prose of those back-page headlines before they become a temporary home for some cod in batter, with plenty of salt and vinegar.

Above all, hold that moment of glory for as long as possible. Mark McGhee again:

> 'I played in a lot of Cup Finals, and I remember that, after the first couple of Cup Finals I played in, the team were taken away to a hotel with the players' wives, and we had a party and all got blootered . . .'

For any non-Scottish readers, it is worth interjecting here that 'blootered' means the same as 'wellied', 'steamin', 'guttered', 'mingin', 'bladdered', 'bazooda'd', 'lummed up' and any number of other variations on a theme. I hope this makes everything abundantly clear.

> '. . . But I learned that it was better that the night of the Cup Final, the day of the game, after the game, these should be times when you take it very easy. Otherwise, you miss too much. You should stay sober, really enjoy it, soak it up and then go and get blootered the *following* night or the following week. It's fine to celebrate in that way, but you've got to remind yourself to take in everything that's happening. You get there at half past one and you have to get out at half past

five, so all that excitement and glory is really crammed into those four hours and you should really try and enjoy every minute of it.'

As Cup Finals go, this year's Scottish FA Cup, in which Rangers decimated Hearts 5–1, demonstrated that, while Juventus had been capable of making them look small on the European stage, in Scotland they were capable of inflicting humiliation on a similar scale on their fellow teams. South of the border, down Wembley way, things hadn't been quite as convincing. Indeed, the English final, despite starring eternal enemies Liverpool and Manchester United, was one of the most disappointing for a while, dull and scrappy, notable only for the single goal that won it for the Manchester side, inevitably coming from Eric Cantona.

It did, however, represent a unique and somewhat depressing record for those supporters old enough to remember clubs other than Manchester United winning things: it was the first time an English club had won the Championship and FA Cup double *twice*. Even if they don't do it again (and, much as I hate to admit it, they still might) there isn't much left of the century to go and it looks as though they have pulled off something unlikely to be replicated while there's a 19 in the year.

And, in writing a book like this, it represents the dawning of what may be an awful truth: if you want to succeed as a manager in today's game, you have to be *Alex Ferguson*. Or at least someone very like him. Yes, while Manchester City fell from the Premiership, the tears of their fans were made worse, a million times worse, by news that Ferguson's Manchester United had become the season's top dogs. Govan's most famous export since Rab C. Nesbitt was on Cloud Nine. Or at least, given Fergie's perpetual grimace, Cloud Seven and a Half.

I did not interview Alex Ferguson for this book, though Mark McGhee, who has played under him and who is a great admirer (indeed, given Mark's ambitions, Ferguson could even be seen as something of a role model for him), has given some insights into his approach throughout these pages. Strangely enough, our paths did cross at the baggage carousel at Heathrow Airport, where the Stretford End supremo had been phoning for a taxi in a state of some annoyance, only to discover that the driver was waiting for him outside the terminal. Newcastle had been booted out of the FA Cup by Chelsea that week, so I wasn't in the mood to try and strike up a conversation, and I imagine I wouldn't have got far if I had. All I can say is that, unlike his erstwhile nemesis, Kenny Dalglish, who apparently possesses a hilarious sense of humour behind closed doors, my short experience of seeing Fergie go about his everyday life suggests that when Steve Harley and Cockney Rebel sang 'Come up and see me, make me smile', Alex Ferguson is not who they had in mind.

Most supporters are, to put it mildly, not too fond of Alex Ferguson (indeed, in popularity contests, he's probably not far ahead of the other Fergie – the one that used to be the Duchess of York). But this is supposed to be an objective book and so we must acknowledge how successful he has been and look for clues as to why this might be the case.

Away from the emotional heat of the season, you have to say that many things about Ferguson's management are admirable. When players at his club were getting old and moving on, he supervised the coaching of a new generation of youngsters to rival the Busby Babes. The early part of the season, with the loss of three key players and Cantona suspended, he both rebuilt and consolidated a side, almost at once, that went on to win the Double.

Kevin Keegan's Newcastle side relied on brought-in talent. Maybe in the future Sir John Hall's vision of a team full of Geordies would be possible, but in terms of bringing younger players up through the ranks, clubs like Manchester United and Liverpool currently seem far ahead (the same being true of Celtic, north of the border). It was the purchase of Faustino Asprilla which many have blamed for the decline of Newcastle's season. My own view, echoed off the record by some of the managers with whom I spoke, is that this purchase was a good long-term move, but a disastrous short-term one. When a player of Asprilla's quality becomes available, you really have to snap him up there and then, as Keegan did. Unfortunately, to keep him happy, which also becomes necessary, you have to integrate him into the team there and then. This occurred late in the season, upset a successful system and probably contributed to the side losing their grip on the Championship. Ferguson, having spent much less in the season, had made a virtue out of a tight budget. He achieved a consistency of style Keegan couldn't. In the longer term, however, Keegan still had the potential for getting the last laugh.

In terms of further admirable qualities, I think Ferguson shows tremendous loyalty and support to those players he admires and to those who reciprocate the faith he has in them. While everyone waited like vultures for Cantona to explode again (myself among them), the Frenchman did nothing of the sort and had an exemplary season. This is unlikely to have been possible without Ferguson's support – indeed Ferguson's conviction that he could revitalise his career with Manchester United when most of the smart money was on Cantona leaving the English game for good. He has shown this kind of loyalty to many other players in difficulty, if what is said about him is true – Lee Sharpe being another who springs to mind. The other side of the coin, however, is that those players with whom he has serious disagreement are unlikely to last long, Andrei Kanchelskis being a case in point.

Ferguson is, however, the kind of manager who, in the words of Mark McGhee, *has to win*, and, when he doesn't, comes across as the poorest of losers. He's not averse to gamesmanship, successfully intimidating Kevin Keegan in the final stages of the season, as discussed in chapter fifteen, by belittling Newcastle's opponents. He knows which buttons to push, having an extremely good understanding of his players – not just of his own but, it would seem, those in the game generally. It's hard to deny that this seems to make you successful. What it doesn't make you is popular, and I wonder whether it makes you happy.

Psychological research suggests that intensely competitive adults who have to win in everything they do are more successful in their careers, but frequently report themselves as less content with their lives. Competition becomes a hunger that can never be satisfied. Either you have to beat everyone else or, if you have succeeded in doing that, you have to continually defend your position at the top from those determined to beat you. This seldom does much to foster satisfaction or contentment.

I thought about this when reading a newspaper interview with Ferguson in which he described the joy he feels when his team win a Championship. The article suggested – and he may have been misquoted – that the pleasure lasts a very short time, perhaps a minute or so, and then it's on to thinking about next season and the problems and challenges that lie ahead. Victory may be fleeting, but *that* fleeting? Does the man never enjoy himself? Perhaps, if you want to win everything in sight, you *can't* enjoy yourself for long.

Liverpool's Roy Evans and Newcastle's Kevin Keegan come across as *nicer* people. But is being a likeable bloke something which gets in the way of winning? Is it something British that playing the game, taking part, and all that Corinthian stuff actually make heroic defeat seem somehow nobler than humourless, carping victory? You can, of course, take it too far and end up with sporting heroes who are a bit of a joke (Eddie 'The Eagle' Edwards, Frank Bruno), but perhaps there is something in it. The Scots still sing of Culloden and remember the 1978 World Cup in Argentina in which, against all odds, they beat Holland, but not by enough goals to keep themselves in it. Mind you, they also sing of Bannockburn, so the odd victory here and there is nice to be going along with.

If Newcastle fans can take anything from what happened this season, we can at least be proud that Kevin Keegan never 'did a

Fergie' and dared to suggest that Man United's final match of the championship would inevitably be a walkover because Middlesbrough fans have never liked their Geordie neighbours and Middlesbrough's manager used, not so long ago, to be Man United's captain.

As Jim Smith put it:

> 'With hindsight, Kevin Keegan's words about Ferguson, even if they won him sympathy, are something he regrets. It's a hazard of doing your interviews with the media immediately after the match has finished. Managers have had exchanges like that in the papers in the past, but this was a big one, and you have to say that, looking back, if his comments *were* a deliberate attempt to unsettle Newcastle, it was Fergie who succeeded.'

He did that, right enough. The Toon were left with honourable defeat.

Honourable defeat. It's not much. Every single neutral fan in the country might have wanted Liverpool or Newcastle to stop the Red Devils in their tracks, but it was not to be. Liverpool's youngsters might have seemed more carefree and spontaneous when profiled on television before the FA Cup than their Manchester equivalents, who looked a little too disciplined and a little too deferent to be true. But the Liverpool fans' exuberance was for nothing. Instead, Kevin Keegan's hair turned a bit greyer. Roy Evans' had already been that colour. Nice guys seldom win, seemed the message.

But there's always next year.

Not that Man United will go away. Ferguson made a few rare television appearances in which he announced, among other things, that he was planning to take up the piano. Whether it was true, or whether it was another game he was playing to enhance his public profile prior to signing a new and lucrative contract is for others to judge. He's going to be around for a few years yet, if not on top of the tree then somewhere very near it.

In the close season, Fergie and Kev ended up sitting next to one another as studio guests commentating on Euro '96. Furthermore, they were even pictured smiling at one another and, if not actually kissing and making up, then doing the next worst thing, as Keegan jovially mimed throttling his adversary. I almost felt disappointed by this show of togetherness. Perhaps the fans need to cast Fergie in the role of football's bogeyman in order to feel superior about a team which, more often than not these days, wins everything in sight. And perhaps Fergie is only too happy to let them.

Meanwhile, Manchester City faced life in the First Division. It would be hard. If the club could hang on to the talents like that of Georgi Kinkladze, it stood a good chance of an early return to the Premiership. But even one season out of the big time is humiliating when everyone focuses on what's happening down Stretford way. As the song says, you can never get used to living next door to Alex.

18: At the End of the Day

'Regrets? I've had a few . . .'

Frank Sinatra

And so another season closed, not the season I had hoped it would be (with Newcastle winning everything in sight) but then when is it ever what you had hoped it would be? Many of the managers interviewed in these pages had also found heartache, and, as Mark McGhee pointed out, many always will. There can't be too many winners, and all the others, one way or another, have to be losers.

For McGhee himself, it could not have been the most satisfying of seasons. For the second year running, a club he had left to join another reached Wembley for the play-offs final that would determine whether they would receive promotion to the Premiership. Unlike Reading the previous season, however, Leicester City made it, thanks to a spectacular, even Cantona-esque, goal by Steve Claridge in the final seconds of extra time. 'Are you watching, Mark McGhee?' was the chant of the fans (now on the way to becoming a Wembley standard).

But you can't look back on what might have been. To be fair to Mark, he had been instrumental in putting Leicester in a position to qualify for these play-offs in the first place, and the fact that Leicester had just scraped their way into them had made fans critical of McGhee's successor, Martin O'Neill. Now O'Neill was a hero and would remain so just as long as Leicester remained in the Premiership. He'd be under no illusion as to how fickle fans can be. From zero to hero was the present verdict, but in no time at all he would be fighting to make sure it wasn't reversed.

McGhee had gone to a club with more potential, a more gigantic sleeping giant, but, by the end of the season, it was still sleeping. Meanwhile, an end-of-season party at Ayia Napia in Cyprus, organised by Mark Rankine, and involving nine other Wolves players, attracted press attention as, inevitably, late-night drinking apparently annoyed other residents. If we can believe the quotation in the *Daily Express*, Mark said: 'It sums up the attitude of most of the squad and I'm not surprised by it.' What was in no doubt, however, was that there would be considerable change among the playing staff. Even Alex Ferguson's son, Darren, was rumoured to be scared about whether he'd retain his place, while John De Wolf found he was one of de Wolves no longer, being given a free transfer at the end of the season.

These were frustrating times for an ambitious manager, but that burning desire to go to the very top of his profession is sure to drive him on to greater glory. What price promotion for Wolves next season?

One team they'll be battling against will be Crystal Palace. Palace made it to the play-off finals only to be beaten by Leicester and that final-minute winner. This book would have read much better had Palace won, of course. Then I could have started on Dave Bassett's optimism and finished on what it can achieve. Still, they came close, and football is rarely the fairy tale story with all the loose ends neatly tied up that you can produce in a work of fiction. I don't think Palace fans could have any complaints about the way that 'Harry' had turned their season round. Like Wolves, however, they would have to wait till next time.

It wasn't all doom and gloom. Jim Smith's Derby County won automatic promotion to the Premiership, finishing second in the

First Division, behind Sunderland. It is interesting and probably significant that, of the two clubs who got promoted straight away and the two who battled for the final promotion place in the play-off final, all four had new managers – it was Peter Reid's first full season at Sunderland, Jim Smith's first at Derby, and both Dave Bassett and Martin O'Neill had joined their clubs in the middle of the season.

I asked Jim Smith for his perspective on how things had turned out.

> 'Obviously, I came with one aim in mind, and that was to achieve promotion. So, happy as we are about it, it wasn't something that made me surprised. I was brought in to do that job, I believed I could do that job and, as long as you get the breaks and get the support – which I have received from everybody, that's to say the chairman, the supporters, players and staff – you feel you can do it, and that's what happened. Without a shadow of a doubt, when you have a new manager joining a club, there's new impetus, new people around, players trying to prove that they can play well to a new boss. Those who work with the players, Peter, Dave and myself, are similar kinds of guy in terms of what we want football-wise and how we want the players to work.
>
> 'I think it's often the case that if you can have the right personality, your first year is often the best chance you've got of making a team buzz. Building up relationships with players quickly has always been one of my fortes. Saying that, there are always going to be some players you can never get any rapport with, but in the main I can get to players very quickly and, more importantly, to all the office people. It's a very open management style that I have and we're all one big team.'

I suppose that, in a nutshell, is what it's been all about: a warm rapport with the chairman; an approachable style of leadership; the ability to communicate effectively and, above all, quickly. Easy enough to remember, but much harder to put into practice.

For Jim Smith, it had been something of a personal victory, too. The previous season, he had been dismissed by Portsmouth, and many thought he might retire from management altogether. His replacement, Terry Fenwick, an ex-player new to management, had not done very well at all, despite the fact that one manager told me he had come highly recommended by Terry Venables himself. Portsmouth had been fortunate to escape relegation, only an extraordinarily lucky couple of defeats for other sides on the last day of the season saving them from such an embarrassment. There must have been a sense of personal vindication in Derby's success. Of his first year at Derby, Smith told journalists:

> 'I was not chairman Lionel Pickering's first choice. Fortunately, the club's other three directors persuaded him that I was the man. My appointment did not exactly excite Derby's fans either. A lot wanted a Steve Bruce-type player-manager. But isn't it funny? Managers who have been successful this year have been the experienced ones. Winning promotion is a dream come true.'

I was keen that he elaborate on this, particularly as England's appointment of Glenn Hoddle had been one where youthful enthusiasm seemed to come above experience. It's true that Mark McGhee and Tommy Burns still had to see their ambitions realised (though the latter already had one Scottish Cup under his belt). What were Jim's views on the fact that, like policemen, managers seem to be getting younger and younger?

> 'Football, like anything else, goes in fashions. Kenny Dalglish may not have been the first player-manager, but he was probably the most conspicuous recent player to go straight from playing into a top, *top* management job – and

did extremely well! Then everybody thought "Oh! That's the way we can go!" and at a lower level, because of the finances involved, it's obviously cheaper to have a player-manager than a manager and a player. I don't think that, in overall terms, it has been that successful for the clubs. Some people who go straight from playing to management are born to it, because it is a *natural* thing, leadership and management, but others have found it hard because it is very difficult to go from near enough just looking after yourself to looking after about twenty-four bodies.'

I mentioned Tommy Burns' comment that he never ceased to be surprised by the fact that so many club chairmen believe that someone who has had a successful playing career will automatically make a good manager.

'Well, I couldn't agree more. But, to be honest, I'm never very surprised any more by what chairmen think!'

What memories would stay with him?

'Certain games stick out in the mind. Just at the beginning of our run of good results, we went to Birmingham City and we won four–one. That was not only a super performance, but it also told us that we were capable of going on and getting promoted. Then there was our last home game, when we knew that we would have to win in order to be certain of getting promoted automatically. We did win and, I suppose that *was* the highlight.'

But there was other success too. In Scotland, Walter Smith presided over a League and Cup Double for Rangers, but is unlikely to have let it affect his natural sense of equilibrium. Someone who is never too downhearted in defeat may be somewhat subdued in victory, but, in his own balanced way, you could tell he was loving it. Did the impending European Championships and Scotland's part in them (particularly the big match against England at Wembley) psychologically fire up his side in a blaze of patriotic fervour? After all, many Rangers players were in the Scotland side (though, unfortunately for the fans, Paul Gascoigne was in the England side) . . .

'I don't think it affected players that much during the season, but it was always on the horizon. First and foremost, they had their domestic ambitions and it was my job to keep them focused on those. As for which players would be involved in the European Championships – for Scotland or for other international sides – that was more or less known already by the players. It can help you in many ways if you have some players who are maybe doubtful for the European Championships – they can be stimulated into playing better, showing their best form in the hope of getting picked.

'But with the closeness in the championship race this season and the rivalry that has always existed between Celtic and Rangers, the domestic game has been uppermost in the minds of most of the fans, too, and Scotland versus England only second. If it hadn't been so close, if we had had the situation that we did last season, the fans would have been talking about the international games more, because there was less competition in the domestic game.'

It had certainly been less of a picnic for the 'Teddy Bears' than usual, at least as far as the League was concerned (their slaughter of Hearts in the Cup was, it must be said, fairly emphatic). From Tommy Burns' point of view, despite the fact that Celtic had failed to stop Rangers in their tracks, they knew they had come close and they knew that next season would be the one in which Rangers could match their record of nine championship wins in a row. It was one that Celtic were determined no one would beat – particularly not Rangers!

Burns' action was swift. The players were straight back into training again in May, seemingly set to train throughout the usual summer holiday. True, they'd had a short break, but there was to be little of the total disappearance followed by a reappearance looking fatter and more suntanned that traditionally characterises the end of season. Celtic were a team with a mission, and if that meant extra training, then so be it.

This is not something you can simply force players to do and it speaks volumes for how close Burns is to his players that they were so willing to follow the plan. *They* knew how close they'd come to snatching the title off the Gers. With more practice . . . who knows?

> 'Our reputation for playing exciting, attacking football is something we want to add to. We want to improve further. I never saw any cockiness in our team, only assured determination to win the next game. With having lost out in the League and the Cup this year, our determination is all the stronger for next year. Rangers showed that they had the better team this year, but *next year* . . .'

This wasn't the resigned shrug of the 'Oh, well, there's always a next time!' Corinthian attitude to defeat. Tommy Burns clearly meant it. Next season the challenger would be fiercer than ever and, as both managers agreed, that could only be good for Scottish football.

For Joe Kinnear's Wimbledon, the season was successful in the sense that they had survived to fight in the Premiership another season, but disappointing in that, after a couple of weeks at the top of the table early in the season, the side slipped and slipped and found themselves fighting to avoid relegation for most of the second half.

The 'Crazy Gang' spirit seemed to have been completely spent during a difficult time mid-season, when Vinnie Jones came close to being transferred following a sneaky approach from Birmingham City's Barry Fry. Later in the season, some of that spirit was to return, but the repercussions of the Bosman ruling were set to hit a club that relied on the sale of its players for its very survival extremely hard. If the smallest club in the Premiership couldn't afford to give its players lucrative long-term contracts and could no longer sell its players to other clubs for huge amounts when their contracts expired, there were bound to be furrowed brows. The idea of moving the club elsewhere to get better gate receipts was discussed – even Joe's native Ireland was mentioned.

Against this backdrop, team spirit must have been hard to maintain. What could be done in this, perhaps the club's most difficult season?

> 'You just have to keep going. I like to come in with the players on Monday morning and have a pot of tea, sit downstairs with all the girls, which is a good crack, have some breakfast and toast and put the film on. By that, I mean the video of the game we've just played. I collect football videos anyway, and watch them avidly. I have a whole room in my house full of videos of different teams. These are so widely available now, with more matches being filmed than ever before. It's a great way of finding out about your opponents' weaknesses.
>
> 'Anyway, we shut the curtains and settle down to watch the video and I can say: "You played like an absolute prat. Why? This wasn't asked of you. What have you got to say?" We're sitting there, nice and calm. It's Monday morning, we're having coffee and a crack and this is the last time we're going to talk about it. We'll learn from it and get ready to prepare for our next game.'

No more Don Howe and his blackboards in today's game.

'Video is a marvellous thing if used in the right way. You've got to make sure it's not detrimental, because a lot of players get embarrassed when you have to sit through a horror show. You've got to know your players' personalities and you've got to know when they're cringing and holding their head in their hands that you should freeze it – but don't go overboard. You're not in there to take the piss out of them or pillory them. You're there to point out a fact that you want to put right.

'What normally happens at clubs when a player has had a bad game is that they come in and say "I had a stinker" and it's forgotten about. I don't like that. I like to analyse things – I'm very analytical – and ask the player "Why did you do that?", find out and see if I can clear it up, perhaps in training. So, in the end, psychologically, the boy is much better prepared in his own mind. It's a relief. It's been buttoned up inside the player: "I had a stinker, I had a stinker, I had a stinker . . ." That can be like a time-bomb for some of the players. They're looking at me thinking: "Are you going to leave me out? Are you going to play me?" I don't like players who walk around like that. I like to get it all out on Monday morning. That way a player knows. I know teams that will let a player bottle that up all week and won't announce whether he's in the team or not until just before Saturday's game.

'I can't for the love of me work that out. You'll be standing in the corridor just before kick-off and a club won't have named what team they're going to play yet. You'll be playing a team like Liverpool – perhaps it's always been a tradition there – but you'll actually be out on the pitch before a match talking to their players and asking them if they're playing and they don't know yet! How can you possibly get across your gameplan in such a short space of time? Who's going to come up for corners, and so on? It amazes me. I think it's dangerous.

> Well, at Wimbledon, the plan for Saturday's match is firmly implanted in the players' minds on Tuesday morning.'

We have to assume that these opponents are being honest when they say they don't know if they're playing. Gamesmanship around this particular area has already been discussed.

> 'But the enthusiasm is there. Last season, my players couldn't wait to play against the Gullits and the Bergkamps. In the run-up to next season, that keenness will be the same.'

But no one is pretending it will be easy. The 'Crazy Gang' mentality is harder and harder to maintain in a game where survival is increasingly not just to do with your passion on the pitch, but with your commercial infrastructure. Huge gate receipts and extensive merchandising seem unrealistic for a club which, as Joe has said, could easily field eleven players from the Wimbledon area. Some even question whether the old 'Crazy Gang' spirit is really still there, including former manager, Dave Bassett:

> 'The Crazy Gang? That was back in the old Fourth Division! Wimbledon have taken that to the nth degree. I don't regard Wimbledon as particularly crazy now when compared with the Crazy Gang of years gone by. It's been a nice little vehicle for them to modify.'

There are changes ahead, without any doubt. I think it's clear from this book that I find Wimbledon a difficult club to hate in the way that others do. They echo so much of the aspiration of any small club, but have taken them to unimagined heights. I hope that, whatever the changes in the game, Wimbledon, come the year 2000, will find themselves still crazy after all these years.

Which leaves the smaller clubs. Wycombe Wanderers finished

mid-table in Division Two, not perhaps as high as some were expecting. Alan Smith, probably the least optimistic and most wryly cynical of the managers in this book, is unlikely to have been overly upset. He does like to win things, but he doesn't believe in unduly unrealistic expectations. Maybe next year . . .

I asked if he was ever likely to tire of the football manager's life, particularly as he's someone who doesn't need the money.

> 'I don't think that way. I always think, well, what would I *do*? Knowing my personality, I like going out for a drink. I like having a reasonably good time. What would I do if I wasn't a football manager? If there was another option open to me, then I may consider it – if somebody asked me: "Would you like to do this?" But I would be very loath not to do something within sport and football. I wouldn't go out to do anything outside. So until the time comes to make such a decision, I'll carry on. I couldn't play tennis eight hours a day – I play it every other day as it is!
>
> 'I've got another year to go at Wycombe – I signed a two-year contract – and there are very nice people there. I'm getting very well paid for a club of that size. I haven't really got an *aim*. If I'm to be honest, I haven't really got something that's *there* that I'm looking to be involved in. And I don't think it really works that way. I sort of have these little ideas, like I'd like to reorganise this coaching, which I think is absolute rubbish, but I don't think I'm going to get the chance to do that. So at the moment, my aim is to get Wycombe as high as I can next season, and I haven't really got anything above that.
>
> 'You can never really predict at the beginning of the season how it will go. Who'd have thought that Graham Taylor at Wolves or Lennie Lawrence at Bradford would be gone from their clubs so early in the season?'

Come to that, who'd have thought that Martin O'Neill, Alan's predecessor at Wycombe Wanderers, and Dave Bassett, who had been such an influence on Alan when he had been a coach at Wimbledon, should have found themselves playing in the First Division play-off finals for a shot at promotion? Bassett was even managing the club which Smith had left so acrimoniously. It's a funny old world.

Smith continued to review the season:

'But there's no doubt in my mind that what I *have* noticed this season is that everybody is much more geared for success than ever before. When we played at Burnley, the supporters *murdered* the manager, a guy named Jimmy Mullen, who was later to be sacked. They booed him, shouted at him and pilloried him because they thought that Burnley should be the biggest club in England, because their granddads told them, and their fathers told them. Whereas, I think back to when I was a kid, if you supported Fulham, as I did, you just accepted that Fulham would be halfway in what was Division Two. We had no great aspirations. We won some games three–one, we lost some three–one. It was bitterly disappointing, but you had no aspirations. I think now, what with more television involvement and everything, the aspirations of clubs are *phenomenal*. Everyone's perception of what success in football means is now much greater.

'That'll mean more pressure on managers and coaches, but it should also mean that you'll get better managers and coaches, and it'll be less easy to sack them.'

And it was there, somewhere in the middle of Division Two, that Wycombe Wanderers, like the Fulham of his youth, had ended up. Who knew what next season held?

And non-league Dulwich Hamlet, under player-manager Frank Murphy, now the wrong side of thirty-five, came close, but couldn't win the ICIS Premier League Championship, which went to surprise contenders Hayes. They were just six points away in a table with little to separate those at the top. For many of the players, it was 'so near and yet so far' again. Non-league football, full as it is of those who came very close to successful professional careers, is permeated with that 'nearly but not quite' poignancy.

However, according to club tradition, a communal viewing of the FA Cup Final was followed by the team holiday abroad, secure in the knowledge that, at this level of football, any drunken excesses, of which I'm sure there were many, would be of no great interest and of even less concern to the manager – or his assistant, coach Johnny Johnson. There are some things going for non-league football! As Dave Bassett observed, it's at clubs like Dulwich where the Crazy Gang spirit *really* survives.

Which just leaves Terry Venables.

Deadlines prevent me from writing more about Euro '96, but as I type, England have just been beaten by Germany in the semi-finals thanks to that cruellest of tie-breaks, the penalty shoot-out. No real fan will blame poor Gareth Southgate for his miskick and all will agree that this was the tournament where Terry proved his critics wrong.

Tabloids depicted tableaux of their own hacks being beheaded as traitors for ever doubting or criticising the man they were now recommending for a knighthood and throughout it all, Terry, like Walter Smith, didn't go overboard over the highs or sink into despair over the lows. His sense of humour and his determination to ignore criticism from those he did not respect served him well. Watching the tournament was like having another little season all over again. So many of the themes from this book emerged. While I went to Scotland's matches and followed the Czechs avidly on television (didn't *they* do well?), England's performance captivated me, as I'm sure it did everyone else.

There was being able to switch off and keeping your cool after an indifferent early result against Switzerland, the growing rapport and team spirit in the side, now that Terry was able to spend longer with them than before and the sense of collectivism, even down to admitting mutual responsibility for any damage that might have been caused by high-jinks on the way back from the team's Hong Kong tour. As I sat at Villa Park watching Scotland beat Switzerland, England's four–one decimation of Holland nearly assured the Scots' progression to the next round. It was the first and probably last time that Scots fans were heard, albeit very quietly, to cheer an England goal.

Some of what I've heard about what happened on the flight back from Hong Kong cannot be revealed here, as airlines have far better solicitors than I do. Suffice to say, mutual responsibility for what went on should perhaps have stretched rather further than just those in or connected with the England team. On the team's night drinking in Hong Kong, however, Terry had this to say:

> 'If the press want to blame someone, why don't they blame *me*? I was the one who let the players have a night off and go out for a drink. Some continental teams serve wine with every meal and let their players have a few beers, too. My philosophy is not to allow players to drink in the run-up to a game, but after we'd played China and Hong Kong, there was a gap and so I let them go out and have a few. You shouldn't blame the players. They didn't break the rules. If the papers want to blame someone, it should be me.
>
> 'Having said that, I think this England side drinks less than any before it. Many of the players don't drink at all.'

Of course, if it hadn't been for England's shaky start, the papers wouldn't have made such a big thing of it and none of them are going to blame Terry *now*. Many of their own reporters spent an extra day or two on the booze in Hong Kong after the team had flown back! All I can add is that I have it on good authority that the Czech team spent a good few nights of the tournament bevvying until the early hours and look how well they performed!

Keeping injured players motivated, managing expectations realistically while the rest of the country went wild, and ignoring ludicrous superstition as Chris Evans and other people paid to talk at great length about the stultifyingly trivial went on and on and on about grey (or possibly indigo) shirts, also formed part of the manager's tasks ('Shirt colour is irrelevant. They'd have played with the same passion and quality if they'd had the three lions stamped on their bare *skins*!'). His techniques for getting the best out of the mercurial Gazza all worked like clockwork and who can forget his expression as he commiserated with Gareth Southgate and tried to reassure him that such a miss can happen to anyone?

'All you can do when someone misses a penalty is to remind them that it can happen to the best of players,' Terry maintains.

Italy lost the 1994 World Cup on penalties. No one goes on about that. While the media made much of Stuart Pearce scoring from penalties after failing to do so in very similar circumstances in the 1990 World Cup in Italy, he had been scoring them for his club side for six years (unlike Chris Waddle, who, it seems, only tried it again once and missed again). Gareth Southgate, a sensitive player, inclined to worry, should be reassured that no one begrudges him what happened. If it can happen to Baggio, it can happen to us all. Afterwards he turned down a huge sum from a paper to tell his story.

> 'I think *any* player would do that. It's one thing to agree to give your story of a match to a paper *before* the game is played, but after something like that has happened . . . well, I can't imagine any player doing it.'

What did Terry feel about the fact that so many matches in the tournament had been decided on penalties? Was it really the fairest way?

'The Golden Goal idea certainly didn't work very well.

Previously, if someone scored in extra time, the other side would attack fiercely and try and get one in themselves. Knowing that the first goal in extra time would be the winner made sides determined not to concede one, so the play became very defensive, and penalties became almost inevitable. They should have tested it out at club level first.

'As for penalties, I think a better method of separating two sides would be to go on some aspect of the game played. After all, if a boxing match is still undecided after twelve rounds, they don't have extra rounds and then a penalty box-out! The judges decide. I think the side that plays the most positive, attacking football should be declared the winner. You could tell that from who had the most corners, maybe the most shots at goal. Still, we all knew the rules beforehand, and you have to abide by them.'

And so Terry's spell as England manager came to an end. 'We came close,' is his final verdict. Glenn Hoddle will find him a very tough act to follow.

Next will come his court cases no doubt, and then I bet it'll be back to the club management that he loves, probably abroad. It is worth pointing out that, while writing this book, my Microsoft spell-checker insisted on continually changing his surname to 'Enables'. Perhaps that has a certain appropriateness to it. As a manager, that's precisely what he does, and the many players he has enabled to live out their dreams will vouch that he does it very well.

I hope he'll still return to the karaoke machine at his club, Scribes, as often as he can. Alan Smith spoke of 'having something else besides football' to occupy your time away from it and keep you sane. Terry has always had such interests, from detective novels to board games to pubs, clubs and everything else. Most salient of all, perhaps are the songs: 'I Write the Songs That Make The Whole World Sing', 'It's Witchcraft', 'You're Sixteen, You're

Beautiful and You're Mine' and, of course, 'That Old Black Magic . . .'

'Down up down up down I go. Spinning around I go. In a spin. Oh, baby, what a spin I am in. Under that old black magic they call football management.'

Epilogue

'Mediocrity knows nothing higher than itself, but talent instantly recognises genius.'

Sir Arthur Conan Doyle

Clive James once remarked that he had read that it was being said that Tommy Docherty was unfit to manage a football team. 'Nonsense!' he commented. 'That's *exactly* what he's fit for!'

To those like James, football management may be the poisoned chalice which anyone foolhardy enough to want it fully deserves. There were times, when writing this book, that I could see why Alan Hansen had spurned the very idea of going into management, preferring instead the role he has adopted as the thinking woman's Trevor Brooking on *Match of the Day*. This, too, has its hazards (Jimmy Hill), but these seem tame compared to the bitterness of defeat, the misery of unfulfilled expectations that litter the Boulevard of Broken Dreams every football manager has to walk so frequently. For people like Dave Bassett or Kevin Keegan, coming so close only seems to make it worse.

Another thing I learned was that even victory isn't always what you were hoping it would be. When I asked Alan Smith what was his most treasured memory in the game, he replied, with genuine sadness:

'I've got to say, there hasn't been one. I thought that winning the First Division Championship at Middlesbrough with Palace would have been that moment. We won three–two and we knew that we'd won the Championship. I thought that was a phenomenal feat. But I remember that, within an hour and a half, I'd got on the train with the players and the coaches and I remember chairman Ron Noades and his brother sitting there – there were no other directors on it – and there was no alcohol, he didn't buy any drinks. I bought some champagne with my American Express card. And then I remember Noades turning to me and saying: "You'll never run the club like you've run it this year. I'm changing it all." So within an hour and a half of the winning the Championship, it had almost been taken away from me.'

Such stories are soul-destroying. But then, Alan was able to salvage something more upbeat from these wrecked memories: 'I would say, though, that the biggest thrill I've had is just the satisfaction of honestly producing – or helping to produce – a lot of good players. That's the biggest thing.'

If a simple definition of management is getting things done through other people, then that must be the key – knowing that you've played a part in helping others to achieve their dreams. After all, the best football managers, of which one of the greatest, Bob Paisley, sadly died as this book was being written, were not necessarily outstanding players themselves. They were, however, able to spot genius when they saw it, and help it to flourish. That was their real talent.

There are numerous stories about the great managers using a bit of amateur psychology to get the best out of players. One classic concerns Jock Stein and Celtic ace Jimmy Johnstone. Stein, having watched a disappointing first half performance by the wee maestro, and knowing, through his extensive personal research into his players' backgrounds, that he was very scared of flying, informed him during half-time that if he improved his performance in the second half, there would be no need for him to fly behind the Iron Curtain for the second leg of the match. The inevitable explosion of goals followed and, sure enough, Johnstone never had to make that flight.

Such stories, however, pass into legend because, I suspect, they represent the exception, rather than the rule. When I first started out writing this book, I thought there would be hundreds of examples of such cunning uses of kidology. But I suspect, in reality, they are few and far between. Indeed, as a couple of the managers pointed out, that kind of trick only works once and you have to maintain a good relationship with your players over a protracted period of time.

In the end, what you need is rather simpler: the trust of your team. That, of course, is easier said than done. However, there can be few management jobs where the bonds forged with those you manage are closer or longer-lasting.

In any kind of management, the people side, 'the soft skills', only forms part of it. There is also the professional expertise, 'the hard skills'. To a football manager, these represent knowledge of tactics and team formations, of how to spot vulnerability in the set-up of opponents and how to minimise the weaknesses in your own side, playing instead to its strengths. Someone once said of Alf Ramsey that there's no substitute for skill, but that it is generally a manager's job to find one and Ramsey obviously found one. Whatever this implies about the limitations of the 1966 World Cup-winning England side, it speaks volumes about the effectiveness of Ramsey as a manager.

Yet the managers of old might not have been able to cope with today's changing game and the modern player. Even Sir Matt Busby struggled to handle George Best effectively. As Jim Smith pointed out, to today's players, with their huge salaries, respect for the manager is not the automatic thing it might once have been. A more democratic process of control is needed and, given the sensitivities of today's players, a softer touch. It is interesting to speculate whether some of the great managers of yesteryear would have been able to adapt to the demands of today's game.

Is football management something any skilled manager could do? Probably not, given the depth of tactical knowledge and background required, something commonly held to be available only to those who have spent a good many years in the game. Then again, as was pointed out, some of the unlikeliest people get appointed managers these days, so perhaps someone outside football could do it. How successfully is another question.

The idea many club chairmen have that a good player should make a good manager, scorned by Tommy Burns and Jim Smith in particular, shouldn't seem unusually naive compared to what goes on outside football. After all, good sales reps are always being promoted to sales management and those who perform effectively with computers, as programmers or software engineers, may find themselves managers in the information technology world. Frequently these appointments don't work out, because what makes you good at selling or designing computer software doesn't necessarily make you a good manager – indeed, the roles often demand such different skills and aspects of personality, it's amazing that such managerial appointments are *ever* successful.

The same holds for football. Some, like Kenny Dalglish, have made the jump from player to manager and been a huge success at both, but there are not too many like him. It has been suggested that Glenn Hoddle simple hasn't the experience or expertise needed to take on the England job. Time will tell on that one, but it is interesting that the two most successful managers in this book this season, Walter Smith and Jim Smith, both came from the older tradition of working their way up through coaching and assisting existing managers, rather than being thrown in the deep end.

Good managers are born, not made, according to some. I tend to agree – or at least, *excellent* managers are born and not made. With hard work, you can possibly grow to be good, but not the best.

So, as a psychologist, what qualities would I look for in a successful manager?

Simple things, really. A strong self-belief and optimism. An approachable, consultative decision-making style. The desire to help others achieve their potential. The need to win. Ah, yes. Let's not forget Alex Ferguson. The need to win at any cost is probably a prerequisite of modern management.

One thing is certain – I wouldn't want to do it myself (I *couldn't*, of course, having nothing like the tactical understanding needed). The craze to be a fantasy football manager shows no signs of dying down, but just picking a team and watching those individuals perform week by week seems as close to the real thing as passing Go and collecting two hundred pounds is to real property speculation. Reality management is so much less escapist and so much more like . . . well, *life*. Life, with all its stresses and strains, its disappointments and defeats and blows to the spirit. But also, life with its hopes and dreams, its triumphs and its victories, however large or small.

Several of the managers I spoke to had other strings to their bow, other business interests in particular. Interestingly, while football is a hobby to so many people who do other things for a living, the things that they do are sometimes reduced to the status of a hobby by the few who work in football.

If some of the contents of this book have deglamorised football management, I think it's important to remember that *everything*, singing, acting and certainly writing, has its unglamorous side. Nevertheless, there can still be some great thrills to be had in the job, and I hope that has come through, too. After spending a year looking into the ins and outs of this rare and fascinating profession, I feel I understand it a little better. As for whether I'd recommend it to anyone, it may be my imagination, but I'm sure Terry Venables' hair has been turning greyer over the last couple of years. Many other managers have got white hair, or in some cases, hardly any hair at all. I think that fact speaks for itself.

Maybe it's not all bad, though. 'When I started the England job two years ago, I weighed fifteen stone. Now I'm twelve and a half!' laughs Terry. All that stress is good for your figure, if nothing else.

Don't put your daughter on the stage, Mrs Worthington, runs the song. And if you let your son anywhere near that dugout, you do so at your own risk.

Dr George Sik, June 1996